C.A.R.E.
Courage to Take Action Relevant to Everyone

Building a Better Workplace Starts with You!

CHARLES LOBOSCO

iUniverse, Inc.
Bloomington

C.A.R.E.—Courage to Take Action Relevant to Everyone
Building a Better Workplace Starts with You!

Copyright © 2010 by Charles Lobosco

All rights reserved. No part of this book may be used or reproduced by any means, graphic, electronic, or mechanical, including photocopying, recording, taping or by any information storage retrieval system without the written permission of the publisher except in the case of brief quotations embodied in critical articles and reviews.

iUniverse books may be ordered through booksellers or by contacting:
iUniverse
1663 Liberty Drive
Bloomington, IN 47403
www.iuniverse.com
1-800-Authors (1-800-288-4677)

Because of the dynamic nature of the Internet, any Web addresses or links contained in this book may have changed since publication and may no longer be valid. The views expressed in this work are solely those of the author and do not necessarily reflect the views of the publisher, and the publisher hereby disclaims any responsibility for them. The information, ideas, and suggestions in this book are not intended to render professional advice. Before following any suggestions contained in this book, you should consult your personal accountant or other financial advisor. Neither the author nor the publisher shall be liable or responsible for any loss or damage allegedly arising as a consequence of your use or application of any information or suggestions in this book.

ISBN: 978-1-4502-5065-8 (pbk)
ISBN: 978-1-4502-5067-2 (ebk)
ISBN: 978-1-4502-5066-5 (hbk)

Library of Congress Control Number: 2010912976

Printed in the United States of America
iUniverse rev. date: 11/18/10

From: Charlie

To: All employees

For immediate release

Subject: Urgent! *Conscious Behavior in the Workplace*

100% of the workforce agrees there are many problems, issues and concerns regarding day to day interaction in the workplace.

100% of the workforce agrees the problems, issues and concerns are caused by others.

Building a better workplace starts with you. Conscious Behavior in the workplace will deliver unlimited results.

Please proceed with a sense of urgency......

….and a willingness to be influenced.

Are you concerned about your job? Concerned about losing it? Concerned about not being able to do anything about it? Are you concerned there's nothing you can do to actually make a difference in the workplace? Have you been recently negatively affected at your job? Are you having difficulty finding another? Are you concerned about how you'll be repositioned in the workplace?

In 2004, my answer was yes to many of these questions and by 2006, yes to all of them. Through Conscious Behavior in the workplace I've since reversed this to a resounding no across the board. Not only that, I've become relevant; a "go to" person delivering results for the common good of the company. Teammates are drawn to me, opinions are requested of me and people listen to what I have to say. Toxic negative behavior is a thing of the past. I've been recognized financially too. This is because relevance in the workplace fosters trust; trust as in trusted to deliver results. Trust fosters cost efficient and quick delivery which is the goal of every company.

C.A.R.E. – building a better workplace starts with you! will show you how to deliver the results that will achieve these benefits, how to become relevant at work and why your relevance at work (both inside and outside of your job description) will make a huge difference to the success of your company.

I share observations, case studies and lessons learned throughout my career which began in 1973. It's clear to me if I knew then what I know now, there's no telling the limits of my accomplishments. It's also clear to me what I know now provides the opportunity to achieve unlimited results from this day on.

The results have been eye opening, providing success and recognition to my teammates and great benefits to my company. I've since developed a C.A.R.E. certification training program so others can share in the success. The benefits of becoming C.A.R.E. certified have changed my life for the better.

Charlie

Contents

Preface		xi
Introduction		xvii
1.	A Startling Observation	1
2.	The Motive	13
3.	The Mentors	27
4.	C.A.R.E. Efficiency Assessments	39
5.	Twenty Ways to Become C.A.R.E.-Certified	129
6.	Conclusion	161
About the Author		163
Author's Career		164

Preface

I grew up in New York City, on the "slummy" side of Queens. My family was in the junk business today known as re-cycling. For my allowance, I used to pick metal. I would walk around the junkyard owned by Uncle Anthony (or Ant-nee) and gather pieces of scrap metal that strayed from the pile. At the end of the month, the precious metals that we found; aluminum, lead and copper would be sold to Uncle Mike at a different junkyard. Even though everyone was tough and dirty, I was nice and clean, almost like a black sheep, or the clean sheep. My family was OK; dysfunctional but OK. I inherited my father's demeanor, personality and what I call "perspective humor". One time in the junkyard office Uncle Anthony had a guest. He was introduced as Three Finger Brown. My uncle asked Mr. Brown if he wanted coffee or needed anything. My father asked Three Finger Brown if he should go look for his other two fingers.

I was a sixty's generation person. When I think sixty's I think color, prior to that (the fifties) my memories are black and white. Some of my black and white memories are no running water in the bathroom, helping my father shovel coal in the furnace during his short run as building super (coal made a great strike box for stickball!), polio and of course Mickey, Willie and the Duke. When I start to remember in color I think of Muhammad Ali, the Magnificent Seven, The Beatles and of course Woodstock. I didn't go to college; in fact I can't really remember one thing that I learned in Flushing High School, the same High School my Mother went to. When it came time to think about college, Uncle Anthony was talking with my father about my future; "these kids today go to college to do drugs and to get stupid! Lets send Charles to computer school, it's the new thing; he'll learn a trade". So that's what I did. I have to say there was some merit to that dysfunctional logic from my uncle. I'm not sure where (if anywhere) my friends that did in fact attend college ended up. But I was off to the races. This new trade opened many doors; I was working, in a career! I may have been the first person in the history of the Lobosco name that was working in corporate and I just turned nineteen. My family would never understand what this career is and what I actually do for a living.

"I can't believe you fix computers, you can't fix anything".

"I don't fix them I program them".

"So now you're a scientist?

"No"

A mathematician?

"No"

"What then, and where did you get this sudden knowledge?"

"You work for IBM?"

"No; Excel Plastics"

"I thought you were in computers?"

"Excel Plastics has a computer"

"So what could you possibly do; turn it on and off?

Since 1973, I could never discuss work outside of work. My career was so foreign to everyone in my family; they thought I was making it up! Meanwhile I worked, observed and absorbed. The workplace was my college; marketing, profitability, economics and everything in between was all included in my curriculum.

My career in the corporate workplace seemed to be fine; I was never out of work, always meeting new people and always learning. I felt as if this would go on forever, and maybe it will.

I blinked and then I was fifty. Somewhere along the way, I got a little lost. I was working but I wasn't relevant. I wasn't making anything better; I was just working. I needed to re-assess. I went internal and re-evaluated. I really did accomplish a lot in my career even with my dysfunctional background, and for that I'm proud. I've been treated well in the workplace and now its time to give something back, to make a difference and become a true teammate. I needed to re-invent myself; I needed a strategy.

C.A.R.E. certification is the strategy and I'm truly grateful for the grounded insight obtained over the last thirty five years that has allowed me to develop and implement this strategy.

There's a bottomless pit of opportunity available in the workplace provided you have the right strategy.

C.A.R.E. certification is the right strategy.

I've seen enormous change in technology in the past thirty-five years, but *no* change in our day-to-day behavior in the workplace.
This needs to change.
We need to step up emotionally at work and be more accountable for our actions, behaviors, and contributions. Contributions at work go beyond just doing what we're told. Our conversations, daily collaborations, day-to-day activities,

teamwork, and even time spent at the water cooler—*all* factor into our results and the results of the company. Our companies need us, now more than ever.

C.A.R.E. – building a better workplace starts with you! provides observations, lessons learned, and behavior examples (since 1973) describing what C.A.R.E. is—and what it is not.

I can't guarantee that you'll find my observations and case studies interesting. I can't guarantee that you'll agree with my needed and recommended training. But I *can* guarantee that when C.A.R.E. becomes your motive in the workplace, your career will benefit. Teammates will be drawn to you; you will become a go-to person, and your results will not be tainted due to bullying, politics, or personal agenda. You will be relevant!

Everything I say in this book is based on real events and real people, not on theories, nor on third party research on corporate behavior. Everything is based on day-to-day interaction throughout my career.

There's no doubt that once you become C.A.R.E. certified, your career will blossom and your company will recognize that you are relevant to its success.

I've received great insight from my career, and great inspiration from five mentors on how to have the courage to question everything. To question not as a post-game expert, not from hindsight, not as a soothsayer, but as a relevant teammate.

C.A.R.E. certification works!

Everyone in the workplace will benefit from this book. However, my observations and examples are specific to my field (technology) and my role as a manager and an individual contributor of technology deliverables.

I'm mentoring C.A.R.E. in the workplace, but my days might well be numbered. They're numbered because I'm working alone, at the bottom of the house, where the workers are. There must be more teammates at the bottom of the house who are C.A.R.E. certified. I need help. I need you. We need each other.

C.A.R.E. is Courage to take Action Relevant to Everyone. We know now what it stands for, but what do those words really mean in the workplace—Courage, Action, Relevance, Everyone?

We all show some form of courage in the workplace. Sometimes just showing up takes courage. What about the courage to say no, to ask why? What about the courage to shed your fear, to speak from the heart? What about the courage to reach out for support among teammates, to discuss the issues behind the issues? This is the courage we need to become C.A.R.E.-certified.

The individual contributor is the one performing the actual work. This is *action*. But is the action *relevant*? Or is it just to satisfy a task assigned by someone else? Is your action taken to advance someone else's personal agenda? I'm not saying this is wrong; many times, this is our job. But it is also our job to question. Ask why; determine if the action you're about to take has priority when measured against everything on your plate; know how it will affect others. What is the real impact of this action to you, to your coworkers, and to everyone?

Everyone; this is where the crowd gets thin. Are you executing tasks assigned for your success only? Are you aware of issues problems and concerns that impact your coworkers but are not saying anything about it? Are you "bullied" into delivering results regardless of the impact? Did you make something better today—on a project, in a meeting, at the water cooler, anywhere? Whose back, in addition to your own, are you watching? Are you collaborating? Daily? With coworkers? With anyone?

What matters is delivering results for the common good of the company, but not at the expense of others. Let's be clear: saying yes to every task is NOT promoting C.A.R.E.; siding with the most aggressive actors is not promoting C.A.R.E.; achieving at all costs, at the expense of others, is not promoting C.A.R.E. and spreading toxic behavior in the workplace is not promoting C.A.R.E.

C.A.R.E is Courage to take Action Relevant to Everyone.

Introduction

"Name a candy bar after Reggie Jackson?"

New York City, 1973. The village was cruising, the Yankees were losing (ugh!), and I was a computer operator for Excel Plastics. I was nineteen, fresh out of "computer school" and learning on the job what "data processing" actually meant. By 1975 I had evolved from computer operations to computer programming. I now worked for Ward Foods; they made Chunky, Oh Henry, and Bit-O-Honey candy bars. My programming assignments were to develop product recall and labor distribution applications. I remember walking over to the marketing department to speak to the manager, Warren: "Rumor has it the Yankees are going to sign Reggie Jackson! He's already said that if he plays baseball in New York, someone will name a candy bar after him. Are we going to?"

Warren replied, "What are you talking about?" Warren sent me over to my boss, Al, my first mentor; Al hired me at Excel Plastics and then hired me again at Monroe Group and finally took me with him (once again) to Ward Foods. Al said I couldn't be going around asking questions like that. I had to let Warren do what he did best, and focus on my own programs.

"Name a candy bar after Reggie Jackson?" Al scoffed. "What were you thinking? This is not playtime. It's work. So, work."

Of course they were wrong. Reggie Jackson became a Yankee in November of 1976, and Reggie Bars did in fact hit the market from a competitor. On opening day in 1978, thousands of Reggie Bars were handed out as part of a promotion. When Reggie Jackson hit a home run during the game, Yankee Stadium was showered with Reggie Bars thrown by the fans to celebrate. Standard Brands, the maker of the candy bar, said it was the greatest PR for a product that you could ask for.

Warren never spoke with me again.

It never occurred to Warren that he could present ideas (upward) in his chain of command to benefit the company; ideas outside of his job description . On the other hand, what, exactly, had I been trying to accomplish? So an idea may have some merit—so what? Did I expect to "assign" it to Warren to make happen?

We were two trees unaware of the forest in which we had planted ourselves.

Warren and I had different job descriptions for Ward Foods. Even though he was the marketing manager, we both represented the "bottom of the house," where the workers labored. The "top of the house" was reserved for the visionaries.

We'll never know the potential of Reggie Bars from Ward Foods because we failed to "manage up" the idea. The top of the house never heard it.

Warren dismissed my idea almost instantly. I've had many similar interactions in the workplace after that one: no need to "manage up" any ideas, thoughts, or concerns; no need to discuss our relevance to the common good of the company; just do our jobs. Be the tree and let the forest take care of itself. Thirty-five years later, it's still a valuable lesson learned for me. Relevance at work must go beyond the job description.

After leaving Ward Foods and finally Al Delgardo, I spent time at SwissRe Insurance and at Republic National Bank. Then, in 1980, I began my second career as an independent technology consultant. My exposure and contributions to over twenty corporations has been priceless, but my regret is never choosing to stay and fight; I always just rode off into the sunset once my assignment ended. This was a bad strategy. What good is priceless, diverse workplace experience if I just go from one company to the next and never really make a difference anywhere?

Fast forward to 2005; I was in a site meeting at my company. All the technologists in the building were there. We were listening to a new corporate visionary who was, well, "visioning."

"Nothing gets done in our company without technology. Without technology, the company would not even open for business."

How relevant is that! I thought. *My field is so crucial to my company that without it, my company would cease to exist!*

In the next eighteen months, countless technologists from my company (including that "visionary") were affected by either job actions or impossible relocation demands.

Any eight-year-old could provide the same "vision"—technology is big these days. This "vision" was nothing more than high level corporate rhetoric with nothing behind it. Such a weak attempt at motivation actually promoted lack of trust.

Technology is relevant. Wow, thanks for telling us!

But are we, the people who develop the technology, relevant? Are we relevant to the point that we can question these visions and what's behind them? Or is just our field relevant, but not us? Or have we just lost sight of what our relevance actually means?

When we become C.A.R.E. certified in the workplace, all of our actions become relevant, to everyone.

This visionary was not C.A.R.E. certified. He did not have the courage to take action relevant to everyone. All he had was courage to address his own personal agenda, which he wanted to achieve at any cost. He was dangerous. When you achieve at all costs, regardless of the impact to others, the results will be tainted.

We all want and need visionaries to think out of the box and promote new ideas; we welcome this. However, we need to trust them, too. Even the best of visions will come up short if there is a lack of trust behind the vision.

How do we establish trust? In the workplace trust is established by delivering results, but not at the expense of others. Also by just being truthful!

So the corporation is upside down; entrenched in chaos, lack of results and extreme economic conditions. Who comes forward? A visionary! Great, we certainly need one. However we need a visionary that first takes accountability for at least acknowledging the state we're in. Then presents the plan to get the company back on the right track. Finally and equally important, asks for our help and commitment to stay and fight with him. Then there would be mutual trust. However we're not hearing any of this, therefore we do not trust what we're hearing. We don't question out of fear, therefore we just do what we're told only to blame when the vision falls short.

I refer to this alleged visionary many times. Achieving at all costs is not part of C.A.R.E. However, neither is blind support by us. I question our support; is it really support for these visions, or is it just to stay safe?

We may have questioned and raised some concerns at the water cooler, having noticed that this guy's career was eighteen months here, eighteen months there. Where was his loyalty, his commitment, his willingness to stay and fight? Where in his career have results benefited everyone?

We may have raised these questions at the water cooler, but for some reason failed to take them upward.

We don't work for the water cooler. We work for our company.

"For some reason": this is the target of C.A.R.E.

At the end of the Enron nightmare, there was an observation: "Ask why" was part of the company logo. The idea is that there was, ostensibly, no ceiling; every employee should therefore have always felt that he or she could ask why the impossible couldn't be done.

Ironically, the individual contributors of that company needed, in fact, to ask why when presented with the corporate rhetoric: Why? Why is what we do for a living so complicated? Why is it that nobody knows or understands what Enron does?

For some reason, though, they didn't ask why.

So I again ask; Are you concerned about your job? Concerned about losing it? Concerned about not being able to do anything about it? Are you concerned there's nothing you can do to actually make a difference in the workplace?

Have you been recently negatively affected at your job? Having difficulty finding another? Concerned about how you'll be repositioned in the workplace?

If the answer to any of these questions is yes, read on with a willingness to be influenced. C.A.R.E. certification is the necessary strategy for obtaining unlimited results in the workplace today.

In 2006, I was impacted by the plans of this visionary. I was asked (meaning told) to relocate from New York City to Cincinnati, Ohio. Not only that, but everyone that I interacted with, including superiors and mentors, either remained in New York or left the company.

After thirty-five years of doing what I do best—networking—I was alone. Now what? Why did I go forward with this? What do I do now? Nobody to interact with, certainly no mentors. Just me.

Negative chatter regarding this move was off the charts; everyone felt that management just wanted to get rid of us, so they probably expected us to leave the company and not relocate. Everyone involved was in a downward spiral, as was I—at least initially. Rather than continue down, though, I reversed my attitude, looked back at everything I'd learned over the last thirty-five years, and embraced the opportunity. I became C.A.R.E.-certified in the process.

My first corporate senior, Al from Excel Plastics, told me to be my own job security. My abilities, not the company I worked for, would provide a secure future.

So what would provide me a stronger form of job security: toxic negative behavior or C.A.R.E. certification?

At the end of the day, it was an easy choice. I needed to make my new role in the company relevant. Otherwise, I would be gone, too.

But I needed help; even with thirty-five years of lessons learned, I was still alone and in need of guidance and inspiration.

I am grateful that I've found five mentors who were already C.A.R.E. certified. These men provided such great insight and inspiration that I built my C.A.R.E. certification training program around them. I'm really proud to have spent some time learning about them so that I can share more about them in the introduction and in chapters three, four and five.

C.A.R.E. – building a better workplace starts with you! will make you aware of the urgent need to become C.A.R.E.-certified regardless of your role, regardless of your perception that you're already C.A.R.E.-certified, and regardless of your current behavior in the workplace.

Who's eligible? Who should read this book? Who should follow up and take the C.A.R.E. certification seminar training?

Everyone participating in the workplace today.

A Startling Observation

Embedding C.A.R.E. into our behavior in the workplace is desperately needed—but doesn't apply specifically to me!

To say I was surprised by the comments and opinions from co-workers when I discussed my concerns in the workplace is an understatement. I was really dumbfounded by the consistency of the feedback, which seemed to say that C.A.R.E. certification in the workplace is urgently needed, but it does not apply to any of them. There has been total denial from *everyone* I've spoken with! When it comes to each one of us as individuals, embedding C.A.R.E. into our behavior in the workplace is desperately needed, but we don't think it applies specifically to us!

It seems problems in the workplace, the current state we're in, the negative chatter and the lack of individual accountability is just the status quo. There's nothing we can do; all of the above (and then some) is being caused by everyone except us!

I beg to differ. Recently, there was another big change at my company, and some of my co-workers were directly affected by it. Unfortunately, they were living in denial that they could NOT have done anything to prevent being negatively affected. To them it's a conspiracy for the superiors to achieve personal gain at all costs; to co-workers, it had nothing to do with their performance, failure to deliver, failure to communicate, become relevant, or adapt to change. This decision by the company had nothing to do with the performance and day-to-day (perhaps toxic) behavior of the individuals impacted. This was done solely for the personal gain of someone else.

Right! We're running out of time. We must proceed not only with a sense of urgency, but also with the willingness to be influenced. Otherwise our days are numbered.

If my days are numbered at my company, I can accept that. Many have gone before me: senior managers, middle managers, people managers, superstars, lead technologists, even visionaries. The fact that I'm still standing only proves further that there's more weight, more value, more relevance to a company from being C.A.R.E. certified than from being a superstar!

There are struggles in the workplace, especially when it comes to managing up. Everything—all the work, all the issues, all the strategies are managed from the top down. We at the bottom need to do a better job managing up, because we are the ones closest to, the ones performing the actual work. Unfortunately, C.A.R.E. is still perceived as a weakness and not a technical skill. Unless I can convince people otherwise, my days are numbered. It's the easy choice: a resource is not delivering, so we need to replace, reorganize, or outsource the function. This has been the plan to the point that there is, at best, very limited subject matter expertise left.

You see, when companies take action, when they downsize, reorganize or outsource, everyone is fair game—the good guys, the bad guys, everyone. This is because we do a poor job managing up. It's on us to make it known to our superiors that *we are relevant.*

Merely replacing a resource that is not delivering will not provide subject matter expertise to the company. My strategy is to keep my team intact, to stay and fight, to apply lessons learned to all teammates (company employees and contractors) so they can become subject matter experts, which is in short supply because of the recent actions taken by so many companies. Subject matter expertise can only be acquired over time; people need time to learn. My teammates are finally starting to get it, and are grateful. But this is new to them, very strange and difficult to accept.

When someone is not producing, regardless if the person is a full time employee or a contractor, I need determine why. I need to raise the bar on this person's performance and not just replace him. Replacing resources more often than not will just perpetuate the cycle of more outsourcing, more off shoring of work and more company downsizing which does not develop subject matter experts, but just new resources. Somewhere along the way people started being referred to as "resources" in the workplace. Maybe this is why it has become so easy to question our relevance, so easy to suggest outsourcing of work to less expensive resources. I couldn't disagree more; people have a heart, a soul, and a brain. All three attributes are priceless when being asked to deliver. I think we need to move away from referring to people as resources.

Honestly, we didn't ask for this. Outsourcing of work is the result of more "visioning" like the one mentioned earlier. But I don't think it's a unique, C.A.R.E. promoting "vision" to travel offshore to a vendor and say, "Share in our success and be a partner." No prior company experience? No problem. No or limited knowledge of our business? No problem. No subject matter expertise? No problem—share in our success and be a partner.

The offshore vendors, of course, say "Okay, no problem; we'll be partners!"

Then they turn the relationship into micro surgery.

"What type of partnership would you like to pay for; fully managed service, staff augmentation, on-site subcontracting with offshore resources, project specific outsourcing?"

I was a contractor for thirty years and it was a lot simpler: do your job or go home.

However since outsourcing is here and it's real, I have to make it work. If that's my task as a result of a command decision, as an employee, shareholder, and customer of my company, I need to make sure these guys are C.A.R.E.-certified. I file that under maintaining the balance between compliance and risk ... and also practicing what I preach.

My team consists of offshore and onshore contractors with no vested interest in the success of my company other than keeping their jobs. At face value, it would be easier to reattach a finger than to expect this group to deliver as a "partner" solely for the common good of the company. However, after one year of C.A.R.E. training, their results have been phenomenal. My team has gone from egocentric, defensive and unaccountable, to being equal to the task of delivery. We utilize C.A.R.E. together as a team to change our behavior, be accountable for our successes and our failures, and work on each project with this passion.

One project in particular is a compliance upgrade. This deliverable has been pushed and pushed to the point that our jobs are at risk. Believe me when I say losing my job for this delivery delay is less of a risk to my company than implementing an incomplete project just to meet the date. Imagine that—

I'm more comfortable with the risk of losing my job than the risk of providing something shoddy. Why? I care! Why the delays? Because I can't get the same level of care from the other supporting groups outside my team. Why? Because that would mean they, too, would be accountable. As long as they can stay under the radar, they will. As long as my job is on the line, I'll be the only one accountable. Company employees blame the offshore contractors; the offshore contractors hide from the conflict. Talk about a catch-22.

So a project is delayed over and over for many different reasons: set the date, avoid the date, delay the date, and pass the blame. But at the end of the day, it's all due to lack of care.

Mentoring C.A.R.E. in the workplace is off far greater value to the company than the tasks or deadlines of the day.

I'm fully committed to these principles. I'm willing to put my job on the line. After thirty years in the workplace, after thirty years and observing toxic behavior in all shapes and sizes in many different companies, it's about time I did something real, unique, groundbreaking, and productive for everyone.

Almost on a daily basis, one of the guys on my team is faced with an issue and the escalation tsunami begins.

My reaction must always be consistent. "Okay, stay calm, and let's discuss." Let's determine first if this issue truly calls for the escalation tsunami. Then let's determine why this occurred, what the true impact is and when we can get it resolved.

I do this before reacting or responding to any escalation.

Meanwhile the bombs keep coming in: What are they doing? Who's managing over there? What the hell is going on?

I ignore these escalations. I first support my team. I keep everyone outside waiting until I'm ready to respond. There are many times—many—I want to say; "this place sucks" but

I remain grounded because I really believe we can improve. I need to convince others by setting the example, ensuring that my teammates know I'm with them even if it's politically correct to side with the superiors. I need to convince my superiors by doing a better job managing up *and* doing a better job at delivering. However it doesn't matter if the approach is groundbreaking; if I can't deliver, it won't work.

Every manager, not just I, would most likely start off doing the exact same thing; determine the cause, the impact, and the resolution. However, (also most likely) every manager would react to the escalation, many times joining forces with the initiator and questioning the team so that they the manager is "protected" from any retribution. I utilize C.A.R.E. and go way beyond the surface of the issue. I specifically target the issue behind the issue before I respond; this is the difference.

After I finish with my team, I say to the initiator of the escalation, "If this issue changed the status of this project from green to red, from sea of glass to a tsunami with no warning, you are the one accountable! Similarly, if there's an issue with my team and project delivery is at stake, it's on me and not my team. For all you know, I've directed them down this path, so, in the worst case, a surgical strike to me alone would've been a better choice. In the future, please ask my permission before initiating an escalation tsunami at my team."

Yes, my response is the same even if the escalation initiator is a superior.

I encountered one situation in my workplace wherein two guys were escalating via email, reply all vs. reply all. This went on all day, with each response creating more chaos. Still they kept escalating back and forth with no regard to others—just put your head down and keep firing!

They were sitting in adjacent cubicles!

We need to do a better job communicating.

I ask my team; "was anyone aware of a pending escalation but afraid to warn"?We as a team are equally accountable to issue these warnings for the benefit of all. My teammates must understand this, but it's a challenge; they are conditioned to say yes to everything mainly out of fear from the examples set by these escalation initiators. Trust does not exist. Whenever accountability is at stake, they become defensive. It becomes a new world order when they're confronted with teamwork and trust. Initially, my teammates were very leery of C.A.R.E. They even used it against me, saying I'm weak and that I'm the one keeping them from pleasing the superiors; that because of my actions, I'm actually causing these escalations.

I'm taking on a lot here, a huge risk. However, project by project, as my team understands when we act as a team and we support each other, then the results are unlimited!

Using C.A.R.E., I know (or better know) what's going on inside my team. What's behind this escalation? I need to make sure I understand this. It's incumbent upon me to convince (or inspire) my team to speak from the heart and without fear. We need to hold together as a team at all costs, but we also need to deliver. It's also incumbent upon me to explain what accountability means. In the workplace, it means if you hear of an issue, even if it's not your issue, you own it. You may have to get it to the right person to resolve, but until then, it's yours.

Now, after all that, we can discuss the cause impact and resolution.

Some of the underlying issues that are the root cause of this and most escalations are offshore time differences; offshore soft skills or lack thereof; project escalators disguised as project managers; and lack of communication, concern, and teamwork outside the immediate teams. All these will be addressed quickly and early. All these "issues behind the issues" will become obsolete if we're C.A.R.E.-certified.

Have you ever been assigned a task or work on a deliverable that was too complex to understand? I've been working in my field for over thirty five years and never encountered a project or deliverable that wasn't met because it was too complex. All of the delays, cost overruns, and failures to deliver have always been due to the people. We get in our own way: personal agenda, staying under the radar, politics, letting others run with the ball only to hope they fumble and poor planning. When you become C.A.R.E.-certified you will be amazed at how many of these causes disappear!

In my thirty-five years in the workplace I have never seen any business problem that was not solvable.

However, in the meantime we, as a team, still need to deliver!

What's preventing me from delivering? On projects in my control, nothing. Any failure to deliver on these projects is my fault, with no excuses. I'm C.A.R.E.-certified; any failure to address the underlying cause specific to my team and my organization is *my* failure. On projects that go outside my control, though, the plot thickens. The level of success depends on the level of C.A.R.E. from the other participants. Really, that's the intention of this book: to reach out and make others aware of how much C.A.R.E. brings to the table.

But what's the point? If it's kill or be killed, why not kill?

The point is that embedding C.A.R.E into our behavior is *right*. My having done so helps me sleep with a clear head: if I'm affected at work, it's because of *me*, my actions, and not anybody else's—and I can accept that. My having done so allows my teammates to work without fear and with respect. It provides them with examples of C.A.R.E. and not toxic behavior for them to model. I remain grounded to the principles of C.A.R.E. because I believe in them and because of the results I've achieved by implementing them.

Keep this book in your hand and refer to it daily. If you don't remain grounded, your sense of urgency to promote C.A.R.E. will fade before it's embedded in your behavior. You have accountability to yourself, your teammates, and your company to make this change! You will be rewarded both emotionally and financially.

Do not be afraid to stay and fight when the going gets tough. Don't be like that visionary, spending eighteen months here, eighteen months there, in one door and out the other. Establish loyalty; it's a key element of C.A.R.E.

There have been many revisions to my C.A.R.E. certification. I'm a technology specialist from the East Coast, where everything (or almost everything!) is quick. It's been a real challenge to stay grounded and communicate how my career and my life have really improved since removing my personal agenda from the workplace and replacing it with C.A.R.E as the motive.

However, I realized I was writing too much about me. I realized how easy it is to spin back into personal agenda. This is not about me. This is about *us*, the remaining workforce, and how we proceed as a unified team with the sole purpose of making a difference in the workplace, delivering results for the common good of the company and not at the expense of others.

Charles Lobosco

Here we are, at the point of no return. Continue reading with the willingness to be influenced, and you'll become part of the solution. Do nothing, and you'll get nothing in return. Nothing will change—not for you, not for your co-workers or teammates, not for your company. It's that simple.

C.A.R.E.—Courage to Take Action Relevant to Everyonee

Still reading? Good decision! You are proceeding with the willingness to be influenced. You're in it now!

Thank you!

I would like to speak with you! What are your concerns; what influences you? How can we collaborate to expand our network? How soon can you become C.A.R.E.-certified?

The Motive

What's clear to me is C.A.R.E.-certified teammates are hard to come by.

Where do we start?

It all begins with a motive. In the workplace it must be courage to take action relevant to everyone; or C.A.R.E.. This *must* be in your behavior, your DNA. This is what defines you. This is embedded in your character. If you take one thing from this book, it is that *you must C.A.R.E.*

Embedding C.A.R.E. in your behavior is the first priority. There's no need to proceed further if this is not accepted.

I'm a technology manager for a large corporation. I often say, about the efforts of fellow technologists: We can be out for dinner, sitting at a table with a rocket scientist, an astronaut, and the secretary of state—and we (the technologists) get the emergency phone call from work!

I'm not only technology manager, but also a shareholder and customer of my company. As a shareholder, I'm very concerned about the current path of corporate: falling earnings, loss of customers, internal reorganizing, downsizing, and outsourcing of work. I'm concerned about the day-to-day morale of the remaining workforce: *there's nothing we can do; five more years is all I need; nobody cares, so why should I?* I'm also concerned about the future workforce. What incentive do they have to pursue a career in corporate? Where are the examples of accountability and C.A.R.E.?

We need to reverse these concerns. We can accomplish this by becoming individual leaders, through our behavior and our actions; by proceeding with a sense of urgency; by caring and working for the common good of the company. The current motivation in the workplace today has taken us into a downward spiral that must be reversed. Our superiors need us now more than ever.

I've achieved great results reinventing myself and my teams to keep pace with the ever-changing demands from my company or companies. Most of my achievements are a result of my ability to utilize my "soft" skills; communicating, likeability, teamwork, leveraging and by promoting C.A.R.E.

Over the years we've become too engrossed in "hard" skill development—which has in fact made us soft! Hard skills like new software training to stay current or PMP certification. We're too focused on metrics; we need to show more emotion, more passion for our cause, which is the common good of the company. The only way to accomplish this is to make C.A.R.E. our motive.

Of the many that critiqued this book, the ones who don't care laughed, with no acknowledgement of any concern. I would venture to say that these guys would not be reading past the point of no return stated earlier. The ones who actually do care said they agree with the concept, but that it is not possible in today's corporate environment. I get the impression that courage is not

C.A.R.E.—Courage to Take Action Relevant to Everyonee

the issue; it's the idea of any action having relevance for everyone that's the problem. In fact, there were two startling responses from nearly every reviewer. The first was the observation that this call to action never applied to them. The common thinking was there was nothing in this book they needed to apply for themselves; there were no important takeaways. The "it is what it is" situation is all due to actions, directions, and decisions by others. After all, problems in the workplace are caused by everyone else except us, right? The second common reaction was the concern over what the corporate superiors would think. How would they react? Translation: How can I spin my personal agenda into this call to action? How can I spin this so I'm not politically associated in case there's negative feedback?

These reactions were revelatory—and hugely disappointing. My objective while reaching out and sharing was collaboration; I had no political agenda, no hope of pushing anyone's buttons. I did not write a tell-all or express negativity toward any company, particularly my own. I have no desire to tarnish my company's reputation; it has treated me well because I have delivered results. In fact, since becoming C.A.R.E.-certified, I have made it my mission to stay and fight to make the workplace better so the company can benefit from the results.

My objective is to get C.A.R.E. examples and case studies from others at all levels. Most asked to see what I was doing; most asked why; most felt their superiors would react harshly toward writing anything in any book without their permission.

C.A.R.E.-certified teammates are hard to come by.

What's clear to me is how challenging it will be to generate awareness and create a call to action within the remaining workforce today. I aim to change the source of motivation to that of accountable participation. If we fail to care, fail to take action, corporate will be forced to continue down the current path of downsizing the workforce and outsourcing our work. Maybe I'm too late, though. Maybe we're too far removed from caring for the common good of the company. In an effort to remedy this, I'm sending the message to the future workforce as well. If I can create the awareness in them to make care for the common good of the company their motive, to instill upon them the need to become subject matter experts (which can only happen over time) and not just employees, I can change the course of business practices for the years to come.

We've become resigned to blaming others instead of accepting responsibility. This has become our motive. We provide more of the same critique and blame when the corporate superiors have no other choice but to downsize and outsource. Where is our individual accountability? It must go beyond merely accepting every task assigned; it must include our motive for doing so. We must consider the choices rather than acting out of habit or fear.

I'm not ready to concede. I owe it to everyone to leave no stone unturned while trying to generate this call to action. I owe it to my daughter Christen, whom I consider the ultimate teammate. If I have learned anything from her, it's how to be a teammate with unbiased loyalty. Christen spent ten years playing fast-pitch softball in an organization based solely on personal agenda—my personal agenda, in fact. Christen was always accountable for her actions, and never used her political connection to the powers that be to influence her role on the team. I'm grateful to her for this lesson learned, and now I'm accountable to pay it forward.

As a teammate, Christen never judged or disrespected her peers. Of course, she was always under the microscope of other parents, school administrators, coaches, and me; she may not have judged, but she was judged by others, constantly.

I ask you all: why do we judge? What is it within us that make us project as if everything is about us?

Who the hell do we think we are?

In the context of a team, a personal agenda is the single most negative attribute. Suppressing our personal agenda is no easy task. However, once it is accomplished, greater things become possible. Today's workplace is in need of teams with unbiased loyalty to the common good of the company.

There will be many takeaways from C.A.R.E. – building a better workplace starts with you! I'm going to give you three right now:

1. Sunset your personal agenda in the workplace.
2. Proceed with a sense of urgency and a willingness to be influenced.
3. Your only motive in the workplace is care; or C.A.R.E. for the common good of the company.

Change has to start with our behavior.

I want to share some interactions I've had with two co-workers each responsible for different functions. These are not crucial conversations, just normal, everyday communication at the water cooler.

Conversation #1.

Co-worker: Nobody cares more than me, but I've been here a long time and believe me, being a nice guy gets you nowhere. I do all that; I'm friendly, never lie, everyone trusts me. Where did it get me? I'm here over twenty years, haven't gotten a raise since I don't know when! There are people here only a few years who have already been rewarded more than I've ever received. How unfair is that? Believe me, it's not *what* you know, it's who you know.

Charlie Speaking: First off, just getting raises is not why you were hired. You were hired over twenty years ago to perform a specific function. Now, twenty years later, if you're doing that same function, and that function has not gone up in value to the company, any increase in compensation over the years should be greatly appreciated.

Also, being trusted is not about lying! In the workplace, being trusted is about delivering results for the common good of the company. Results can be task or project delivery, but results are also ideas, relationships, participation, opinions, and anything else that will benefit the company.

You're wrong; it's not who you know, it's who you are!

CW: What are you trying to prove? That you're better? You think sweet-talking your way up the ladder will get you more money? What exactly do you accomplish, anyway?

CS: Results, delivery and teamwork. If I only talked the talk and didn't walk the walk, the company would walk me right out.

If I expect the company to show me the money, I should expect them to show me the door!

CW: So what does teamwork mean to you? Do you just delegate everything out to everyone else, accepting the praise when you're successful and passing the blame when you're not?

CS: As a teammate, I am part of a team, no matter if I'm the putative "head" of it or not. I'm a hundred percent accountable for my actions and the success of the team. What's delegated and what's not is a team decision.

CW: Oh, a perfect world. Well, it doesn't always work that way. All I know is I'm here over twenty years; I must be good at what I do. I put in eight hours a day and then some. If they want me out, they have to give me a package; after twenty years, it's the least they can do.

CS: This reeks of hostage ball. Have I ever told you about that?

CW: Nope.

CS: I was a Junior Olympic fast-pitch softball coach for ten years. Early in my coaching career, some of the parents of the more talented players were making demands and dictating who should be playing where and when, threatening to take their kids and go elsewhere. I thought of it as "hostage ball."

I thought, *The Yankees don't print the player's names on the uniforms. Why? Because no player is bigger than the team.*

And now I know it's the same in the workplace: there's no room, no time, no place for hostage ball. Not now, when the bar needs to be raised just to survive. Maybe it was accepted in the past, but not any more.

The above conversation clearly identifies the problem: we, the workers! We have a stalemate. Who listens to whom? This is the issue, not the work itself. We have failure to communicate, failure to collaborate. We can produce the most complex hierarchical schematics conceivable, but they will all be meaningless if we're not on the same page with regards to C.A.R.E.

How can a twenty-year person say this? Twenty years; that's 7300 days! How can you not be part of the problem—how can you say, after 7300 days, that it's everyone else? How, after 7300 days, do you not know the right people? How, after twenty years, can it be that the best you can come up with is, "After twenty years, if they want me out, they have to give me a package"?

So we have a situation where corporate needs us now more than ever, and our strategy is hostage ball! Instead, we should proceed with a sense of urgency and the willingness to be influenced.

So why is my co-worker still here, particularly when so many have been let go in the last three years of downsizing, reorganizing, and outsourcing of work?

He's here because he's doing his job, that same function for the last twenty years. That's a good thing!

He's also still here because the company (for now) is tolerating his (toxic) behavior, probably wondering if it's spreading to others—which it is! Perhaps they're just too busy themselves even to notice.

Why can't he embrace his functional responsibilities at face value and leave it at that? Why all the negative chatter about being passed up? What good are twenty-plus years of hard work if you can't support someone other than yourself being rewarded by the company?

Let's continue the conversation.

CS: Let me give you an example. Our latest release included some reports that were "compliance specific." These reports affected many development groups. When I reviewed these as part of the release requirements, I asked, "Why not track the compliance-specific reports outside of the release instead of coupling compliance deliverables with a generic software release? It overloads the developers with this deliverable, especially when, according to the requirement, the reports are quarterly and the next release is targeted for delivery in November." After some discussion, this eventually occurred; the reports were pulled from the release and tracked separately.

This decision had an overall positive effect, and all it took was for someone to observe and speak up.

CW: Pffft, they don't care. This happens all the time—overload the developers at all costs just to make the release date. You got lucky! You went to the right people.

CS: I know the same people as you. All I did was mention the concern.

CW: So what's your point?

CS: I didn't just say yes to the requirement; I questioned it, leveraged lessons learned from other deliverables, and was able to pare down the effort, which enabled everyone to meet the release date. That's something you, with all your years of experience, could have also done.

CW: Ha! There's no way I'm going to suggest something like that. I'm not putting myself on anyone's radar. I've survived at this place for so long because I know when to keep quiet. This release issue that you brought up did not involve me, so I just sat back and did what I was told.

CS: Well, it didn't directly involve me either. However, it involved my team, and as a teammate, I was concerned.

CW: If I was your superior, I'd tell you to mind your own business and do what you're told.

He got the last word because I didn't know what else to say. This was not a conversation about who's right. It was a conversation that described two different workplace views on C.A.R.E.

What's really interesting is that the co-worker originally said he does care; it's everyone else who doesn't. Over the course of the conversation, though, he proved himself to be one of "them" after all, not caring and not willing to be influenced, just passing the buck up the chain of command to his superiors.

Conversation #2

Project Manager: If you don't provide your updated release sizings to include the compliance reports, I'll be forced to escalate.

Charlie Speaking: I don't believe these compliance reports should be tied to a release. They should be tracked and delivered separately.

PM: I bet many would agree. However, the requirement is to include them.

CS: Did you question this?

PM: My role as PM is to manage the metrics, accumulate the project artifacts, and move the project along. If anything prevents this, I escalate.

CS: Are you a project manager or a project administrator?

PM: They're one and the same.

CS (thinking, *No, they aren't*): Anyway, I was able to make the case for uncoupling the compliance reports from the release. Therefore, my initial release sizing still holds.

PM: Whom did you make the case to? Maybe you want *my* job!

CS: I made the case through my chain of command, and they supported the decision.

PM: If you're going to undermine my authority, I'll go on record that you're not being cooperative. I'm not putting myself at risk because of your desire to get out of doing some work.

CS: I'm not undermining your authority. As a teammate of those who are part of this project, I felt the need to get this effort pared down for two reasons: there's no need to overload the release and put delivery at risk, and these compliance reports are not needed until next quarter! It made no sense to include them.

PM: If the superiors wanted them included, they're to be included.

CS: The superiors suggested it, but it's up to the project team to confirm.

PM: If you're going to question everything, we'll get nothing done.

I left it at that and moved on. I'm not going to judge. The PM, like the coworker, was not willing to be influenced; they were not interested in the concerns of the team; they're not promoters of C.A.R.E.

In the scheme of things, these may appear to be two meaningless conversations, but they're not. They show the day-to-day behavior of the individual contributors in the workplace—behavior that, in order to achieve extraordinary results, needs to change.

Can this book convince these guys to C.A.R.E.? If the answer is yes, this is by far my greatest contribution to the workplace. This far exceeds all my project deliverables over the last thirty years. If not, if workers will not change the day-to-day behavior because everyone is in denial, I offer a suggestion to them all: continue with your functions, continue doing your job, but embrace the support received from co workers who are C.A.R.E.-certified.

So you don't want to be C.A.R.E. certified; fine. Accept the support of those who are. Don't spin it, don't critique it—just embrace it. I believe that you will see examples of teammates with whom you will want to work, instead of merely being forced to work.

How will you know when someone is C.A.R.E.-certified?

Good question.

My co-workers in both water-cooler conversations would swear up and down on the corporate bible that they're C.A.R.E.-certified. But they're not, certainly not by my standards. Where is their courage to take action relevant to everyone (or anyone, for that matter)? What are they making better? Whose back are they watching besides their own? Their actions and behavior are completely consistent with every other person I've spoken with regarding C.A.R.E. They all think the issues, problems and concerns in the workplace today are caused by everyone else!

I want everyone in the workplace to become C.A.R.E.-certified. I want to see everyone in the workplace wearing the C.A.R.E. certification pin. The pin is given after completing the C.A.R.E. certification seminar. The pin is not given by me, but by the attendees of the seminar. This is not something to take lightly. C.A.R.E. certification is *earned*; those who participate certify each other as the final proof of their commitment to C.A.R.E.

My vision is to walk into a conference room and immediately see who the C.A.R.E.-certified co-workers are. The pin will identify teammates who have the courage to take action relevant to everyone.

What are the benefits? Your job will become relevant to the common good of the company. You will realize that you can make a difference: you can reverse the current path; help secure customers and their satisfaction; slow, stop, reverse the outsourcing of work; even bring back former co-workers.

What are the risks? Unfortunately, there are some. Let's face it; it's a jungle out there. When you lead with C.A.R.E., someone will try and take you out. There will always be a price. Look at the above conversations; my co-worker interpreted C.A.R.E. as nothing more than being a nice guy and teamwork as nothing more than passing the buck. He did not show a willingness to be influenced; he's now promoting his version of events via negative chatter, spawning all kinds of toxic behavior. The same is true with the project manager. Whether it's leadership through behavior or leadership by title, there will always be a price. I'm paying a price by writing this; I might be left on my own if it turns out to have negative impact on my, or any, company. What drives this? If it's not about us, about our own personal agenda, do we really care what goes on? I'll go one step further and ask; do we really care if anyone besides us becomes successful or makes anything better?

The Mentors

Find a mentor who is C.A.R.E.-certified.

When C.A.R.E. is the motive, nations can be raised!

Let this sit for a moment; let it resonate. This is a priceless lesson learned from my mentors: Sam Adams, Paul Revere, Thomas Paine, Patrick Henry, and George Washington.

In 1775, these men took it upon themselves to raise a nation. The objective was liberty. The motive was C.A.R.E.

How is it possible that I had to go all the way back to 1775 to find mentors for how to improve conditions in the workplace? All my mentors, the people I wanted to be like, the people I viewed as successful—all my mentors came and went. I was getting tired of changing. I really needed to get as far away as possible from these modern-day visionaries who wander through the business process with no foundation, no life-long commitment or accountability, just high level rhetoric the likes of can be provided by an eight-year-old.

At the time, these five men were not official elected leaders; in 1775, this country had no leaders. They were people managers and future leaders in title but at the moment individual contributors at the bottom of the house, leading with their behavior; just like me. Their motive was care: to raise a nation. It could have been personal agenda, but all that was put aside, taken off the table. Sam Adams said, "We are not what we should be." I interpret this to mean that, as a nation, we can get to a better place. He could have given up, but he didn't—because he cared. The motive was care: to raise a new nation, to provide each citizen the ability to express himself without repercussions. This took courage.

Though we know them as our founding fathers, these men were not leaders at the time, just ordinary people at the bottom of the house achieving extraordinary results. But they were giants! Their results *were* extraordinary!

Where would we be today without them?

When care is the motive, nations can be raised.

These men raised a nation! Their common motive was care.

Imagine what we could accomplish in the workplace if we shared this motive, if we all had this courage. Imagine the productivity, the morale, the change in the day-to-day conversations. Imagine a workplace where the focus is on the work, on making things better, on collaboration and results, on real teamwork, instead of on individual achievements. Imagine a workplace where the people at the bottom of the house have equal information, equal accountability, and equal rights to contribute and question as those at the top of the house.

Twenty percent of the workforce comprises leaders in title. These leaders in title are leading the remaining eighty percent. However, both groups are ordinary people capable of achieving extraordinary results. Therefore, the remaining workforce must become equal (with our behavior, with C.A.R.E.) to our leaders in title when providing day-to-day leadership in the workplace.

This country was founded on that exact principle; ordinary people achieving extraordinary results.

The people at the bottom of the house are the target of C.A.R.E. – building a better workplace starts with you! I can't tell leaders how to lead or managers how to manage. What I can do is help us understand how to improve what we *can* control: ourselves. I'm not saying there is no productive and needed training on management and leadership available to us today. I'm saying if your motive is personal agenda, regardless of any training, your results will be tainted.

The chain of command actually promotes a negative blame game. I hear the same thing over and over at the water cooler: "My manager is clueless; he's not qualified to be managing people; he was put in this position as a result of a reorg." Dare I add maybe even as a result of a visionary or a mentor!

We can't expect leaders in title or people managers to resolve all issues and we can't expect to hold them solely accountable, either. We can't expect to be successful if all we say to them is, "Tell me what you want me to do." Therefore, I speak to the individual contributors. What can we do to build a better workplace?

When C.A.R.E. is the motive in the workplace, not only your career, but also your life, will benefit. I'm totally disgusted with the day-to-day behavior at the bottom of the house where I live. There's absolutely no reason for all this angst which then spreads from the workplace into our lives. We create this based on assumptions because we fail to communicate; we then spiral downward into toxic, negative behavior.

How can toxic, negative behavior lead to upward mobility in the workplace? How can toxic behavior even provide continued existence in the workplace?

After thirty-five years, I finally got it. If this motive, care (or C.A.R.E.), actually helped raise a nation, why not apply it to the workplace?

This is my "Ah-ha!" moment. This has changed not only my career but also my life. If toxic behavior in the workplace spills over into our lives, the same is true with mentoring C.A.R.E. in the workplace. Once you subscribe to C.A.R.E., once you show the courage to take action relevant to everyone, once you become C.A.R.E. certified, your behavior in the workplace will spill over into your life, like it did for me.

Once my behavior changed, once my personal agenda was gone, great things started to unfold. I began to think much more clearly! Toxic behavior creates way too much internal clutter. Now when my head hits the pillow, my day-ending thoughts are, *Did I make anything better today? If my day was shown on the evening news, would we see someone leading from the bottom? Are my teammates and co-workers safe, at least for the time being?*

I'm new and improved! There have been more accomplishments (and rewards) in the last three years than in the previous twenty! I perform outside my job description working to make my location relevant to the company and not just a site that houses resources. I've inspired my team, which was formed only after I relocated, to lead with character. As a team, we now manage eight production applications for the company at a fraction of the cost prior to 2007. I've learned how to communicate with those who manage me, to "manage up" and promote the relevance of my team. I've become a leader not so much in title but in behavior. Even with all the downsizing, reorganizing, and outsourcing of work, while most of the salaries have remained flat, mine has increased! I'm not just doing my job; I'm making it relevant, and the company has acknowledged this improvement.

There was no conspiracy. The corporate position was always about delivering results. Becoming C.A.R.E.-certified has helped reinvent my career and allowed me to continue to deliver results. This will work for you, too! I have a renewed purpose, a positive outlook on life, which includes the workplace. My attitude is gratitude! I believe in me!

Maybe I should thank the corporate visionary who, in 2004, turned my company upside down to the point that even he fell out through the bottom. Maybe I should thank him because by observing his actions and his corporate rhetoric, I've become the antithesis: C.A.R.E.-certified.

My five mentors (Sam Adams, Paul Revere, Thomas Paine, Patrick Henry, and George Washington) assumed much risk along their quest. Paul Revere could have very easily networked himself right into a bullet. Patrick Henry could have been awarded death for his desire to pursue liberty. Still, they cared about the greater good, and their behavior inspires me.

This is teamwork. Unfortunately, there will always be risk. However, when working within a team that has everyone on the same page, with the same motive and the same objective, there will be a greater chance of success.

Do you have the courage to honestly assess and determine if you are the one standing in your way? Do you have the courage to take the necessary action to remedy that? Do you have the courage to let someone else run with an idea, even if it's your idea, for no other reason than that that person can deliver faster and more efficiently than you? Do you have the courage to change?

C.A.R.E. is my motive, and to that end, I include myself as part of everyone. I must proceed with a sense of urgency and a willingness to listen to others. So how do I make it easier? Promoting C.A.R.E. in the workplace can easily be interpreted as weak, soft, idealistic. Plus, I'm only one person. What do I say, when, and to whom?

I can't tell you; that has to come from you, and it has to be real and from the heart! However, we can defer to our mentors to provide some tools to help build the skills we need to implement our new behaviors.

Find a mentor or mentors. Be careful; don't find a mentor because it's politically correct, find a mentor who promotes C.A.R.E. Ideally, find a mentor who's C.A.R.E.-certified. Before you start contemplating your mentor selections, please take a moment and review mine. They were selected after much research and many lessons learned.

My career as a technology consultant has taken me to over twenty corporations. Corporate evolution has provided many observations, lessons learned, and lessons we're not learning!

During my career, there were too many leaders. My views on leadership were skewed. Maybe, early on, I was a victim of "it's not what you know but who you know" and it had a negative impact on me.

Over time, I realized it doesn't matter who you know.

My early mentors all came and went; I'm the only one left. I needed a mentor who was not a leader, I needed someone closer to the work, someone who does what I do, someone who shares the same common motive: C.A.R.E.

C.A.R.E.—Courage to Take Action Relevant to Everyonee

In 1989 to 1990, and again in 1995 through 1999, I was a technology consultant for Manufacturers Hanover Trust. What I didn't realize back then was that I was part of a great team. However, I was too caught up in my personal agenda. I was a developer, part of a team that developed software to support a series of mergers and acquisitions (which were common during that time). Multiple mergers and acquisitions resulted in one huge corporation, but the subsumed entities all had different processes, strategies, and leadership. Maintaining the individual identities of the customers was accomplished only through the great work by the team. Strategic planning alone does not lead to successful results. Credit needs to go to the efforts of ordinary people doing extraordinary things. This team was quick to deliver, because—crucially!—everyone trusted each other, and everyone shared the same motive.

The technology supervisor in this company was C.A.R.E.-certified. C.A.R.E. was in his behavior and in his day-to-day interaction, which provided tremendous motivation. I remember one time in the elevator when he asked me how things were going. He was watching my back! I, being all doom and gloom, told him I was struggling, working as hard as I could just to keep up. Of course I also said I really needed to excel there; I was financially dependent on the company and couldn't afford to be out of work. He said, "Well, peace of mind is free; all you can do is trust your abilities and do what you can for others. Then, when your head hits the pillow, you'll be proud of your accomplishments."

This is what we need to get back to: collaboration from ordinary people with an eye toward achieving extraordinary results.

If this is not being encouraged by our superiors, we need to mentor ourselves.

How do we achieve extraordinary results in today's corporate environment? The playing field is now changed. Our teammates are no longer home-grown; teammates today come from locations across the globe, with no history or past projects to leverage against future achievements. Examples of true teamwork, especially in the corporate workplace, are hard to come by. Maybe we've become too educated about leadership, so everyone wants to be a leader in title. This motivation has taken us down a path where we seem to care less about the results and more about managing the metrics. This needs to be reversed.

I needed some guidance: a mentor, someone to motivate me, someone who does what I do. I needed a mentor who was C.A.R.E. certified.

I needed to go back to a time when there were no leaders, only teammates, and analyze how leadership evolved from within. My research mimics that of the lawyer looking back into case history to find a precedent on which he can base his defense. I did my research, and I found my mentors.

I can't get past their greatness and ability to rise up to lead when there were no leaders. Their true and common motive was that they cared. No political agenda, no permanent campaign strategy; just honest, pure collaboration committed to the same cause. Truly unbelievable. Together they acted as teammates; when needed, they became leaders. Trust was high, results were fast, and loyalty was crucial.

If any of us believe that we as individuals can't make a difference, think of those five men who raised a nation. Share in the success of their model, and the bar will be raised. These five men were masters of nine components: Teamwork, Leadership,

Communication, Trust, Loyalty, Care, Tolerance, Leverage, and Character. Every one of these components is equally crucial to bringing out the leader residing in all of us.

The wisdom of Samuel Adams, the social energy of Paul Revere, the fight of Patrick Henry, and the drive of Thomas Paine, are all required in every team. You bring to the table that which you possess even as you develop the others within yourself. Then, there's George Washington. I look to him as a mentor from the time when he was just a teammate sitting in a meeting listening to Patrick Henry. He was being tasked with the delivery of liberty! The only way for him to succeed was to find his own way—no metrics template or model to follow. Just find a way!

Leadership is not in our title but in our behavior, in our heartbeat. Thank you! Lesson learned from my mentors.

Earlier I stated three takeaways. Here are two more:

1. Leadership comes from within. There is leadership in all of us. This MUST come out in our behavior; we're all leaders!
2. When the motive is C.A.R.E., teamwork and leadership are one and the same!

Thomas Paine fell in love with this country because he observed the leadership qualities in the people—ordinary people doing extraordinary things. Paine, an Englishman in America for just two years, found it truly a revelation, and it inspired him to write *Common Sense*.

The sense of urgency from the pen of Thomas Paine was also present in the words spoken by Patrick Henry. He was a master of speaking in questions to drive his message. I can hear him today, picturing him in the workplace: *Do we not care? If we do, why do we stand idle?*

Over the years I've seen an increase in hard skills and a decrease in soft skills. My approach to achievement has always been hard work. Not that I don't pursue and maintain hard skills, but I've always leaned on my soft skills. I trust them. We must step up, we must raise the bar. Mastering soft skills does not mean you are soft! Was Patrick Henry soft?

Politics, personal agendas, denial, passing the hot potato, negative critique: all represent the current workplace addictions. It's time for an intervention. I am here to intervene.

I'm only one person, it's true. However, if we think one person can't make a difference, well, we should just think of Paul Revere! One man riding alone through the night effected the change that defeated the unstoppable British invasion from decimating the colonists. He had the courage to take action relevant to everyone.

C.A.R.E.—Courage to Take Action Relevant to Everyonee

One person can indeed make a difference ... as long as his motivation is C.A.R.E.

Do you believe C.A.R.E. certification will make the workplace and your career better? Is it possible? Do you believe Sam Adams, Thomas Paine, Paul Revere, Patrick Henry, George Washington, and I alone have benefited in life and career from being C.A.R.E.-certified, or do you believe this behavior will benefit your career and life?

If you had your own company, would you prefer this behavior in your employees? Would you prefer your employees to be C.A.R.E. certified?

C.A.R.E. Efficiency Assessments

C.A.R.E. Efficiency Assessments are individual (soft) skills assessments using my mentors as a guide.

I have to go back and talk about my mentors on teamwork. Five guys whose only motive was care where results were quick and trust was crucial. I'm grateful of course for their cause but also for their examples.

I can see corporate leaders spinning today: *Sam Adams is too old; we need new blood, fresh ideas. Paul Revere brings nothing to the table. Likeability is not a technical skill. Patrick Henry is too confrontational. Thomas Paine thinks he's working for the tabloids!* If I had to guess, they would probably keep George Washington, but not the Washington I consider my mentor. My mentor exists prior to 1776, when he was just a teammate.

This team is a perfect example of finding leadership from within. If, as a team, we keep our personal agendas off the table and focus on the goals, great results become possible.

This exercise is helpful when recruiting, but also for your own personal assessment. This is when you can in fact apply your personal agenda. When it comes down to you weighing in on yourself, there is no need to be politically correct! Be as (brutally) honest as needed.

Samuel Adams

Wisdom and experience. I refer to Sam Adams as the father of the forefathers. It would've been very easy for him to be bitter, angry, and negative in his behavior. However, he was wise, and observed the world around him with a vision, saying, "We are not what we should be. We should labor rather for the future." Sam Adams did everything in his power to pursue this vision; he certainly tolerated the present, but with an eye to the future. Adams was humble, disinterested in popularity; he did not lead with his ego. In fact, not much has been written about him. Only later, during John Adams' presidency, was much regarding Sam Adams documented and preserved. When I lean on Adams as a mentor I ponder, *Have you been doing your job a long time? Are you far enough into your career to be considered wise? Are you*

communicating, observing, leveraging skills, and seeking the facts with unbiased loyalty to your cause? Are you applying lessons you've learned? This carries great respect. How often are you asked in the workplace, "What do you think?"

Paul Revere

Social energy. I see a lot of Paul Revere in myself. We are not the smartest, or most aggressive; not usually the ones considered to lead or provide direction. However, we are often the "glue" that holds together a plan, cause, or vision. I see Revere as someone who bounced around, endlessly networking, leaving no stone unturned to promote and execute a plan. When I use him as a mentor, I think, *Do you network well? Share in discussions? Do you reach outside your area to expand your network? Does everyone know you at work? Are you likeable?* Likeability may not a requirement in the workplace, but it is certainly a nice to have.

Why do we discuss and refer to Paul Revere whenever the event of alerting the public that "the British are coming" is the topic? Why not William Dawes? Dawes also rode out to alert the people. In fact, he made it to the finish line, while Revere was stopped, and had to continue without a horse. Yet today, we only refer to his role. Why? I believe it's the likeability and also the creativity factor. Revere had creative talent, allowing him to think on his feet in the face of adversity. This skill might be one that wouldn't appear on a resume, but would often be the difference between delivery and failure. That night he purposely did not carry any weapon. When he was stopped by the British, the assumption was he was out socializing! Slick!

Patrick Henry

Commitment. Two hundred and thirty-five years before 2010, Patrick Henry declared, "Give me liberty, or give me death!" Think ahead two hundred and thirty-five years from today; do you think there will be any statements you make on your watch that will immediately identify who you are and what you stand for? This phrase alone gives Henry mentor status in my book. I wonder, *Once you believe in something, are you willing to fight for it? At all costs?*

This one phrase speaks directly to communication, commitment, and tolerance. Patrick Henry had talent not only to reach an audience, but also to reach them with passion. Passion is the key ingredient. Henry used rhetoric, questioning his audience, "Why do we stand here idle?" This is a great technique. When you speak in questions, they have to be answered, which promotes dialogue and collaboration. I keep Henry very close to my mind when I speak. If I have something to say, I say it with passion. I, too, am learning the art of speaking in questions. What is the purpose? Why is this suddenly my priority? When I ask, I ask with passion.

Thomas Paine

Communication. Thomas Paine definitely possessed the power of the pen. His revelation about America was, in my opinion the tipping point, of the revolution. Paine was an Englishman who had been living in this country only two years when it became blatantly clear to him that there was greatness in the Americans around him. He observed the day-to-day actions of the common people, and realized that greatness comes from within not from genetic background or inherited title. He penned *Common Sense* as quickly as possible. He needed to share this, to send out a call for action.

Believe me, I'm no Thomas Paine, but my goal is to accomplish the same—to reach every remaining man and woman in the workplace today, drive home this message, and have the entire workforce bring out the behavioral leadership for the common good of the company. Paine, like Henry, knew how to reach an audience; his pamphlet made quite an impact. The written word can go a lot further than the spoken word. Paine used this leverage to reach everyone. When George Washington read *Common Sense*, I'm convinced he got what I got—that they, like we now, were at a tipping point. Washington utilized Paine's ability to communicate in order to reach the troops. Paine certainly qualifies as a mentor on communication. When I write, I now ensure I get to the point quickly.

George Washington

Behavioral leadership. Trust me; one thing we don't need is another book on the leadership abilities of George Washington. However, my take on Washington is about his life prior to his becoming a leader in title. When I think of him in the early days, I see his stoicism. Stoic observations, stoic participation. He was allowing the likes of Sam Adams and Patrick Henry to state their causes, watching them persuade the people of the need for action. Washington was not the one who led these sessions. He listened, stayed under the radar, and then moved forward with unbiased loyalty to the future of America. Many things have been said of Washington, but when he mentors me I hear him asking, *Do you learn from people? Are you humble? Would you run if you had to, in order to regroup for another day?*

Rarely does a leader prepare a plan to sneak away from the enemy for the sole purpose of living to fight another day. That move, which occurred in August of 1776, makes my hairs stand up. This wasn't surrender or retreat; this was escape, quietly, with the entire army. How many lives were saved that night? On both sides?

Here is a lesson to be learned: sometimes the strategy needs to be that you do whatever you can until a strategy develops. Washington could have fought to the death in New York and still be known as an American hero. Instead, that night he saved himself and thousands of others, and lived to triumph overall. I believe his motive, which was care for the common good of the future of America, is what carried him to these unbelievable actions. George Washington was a teammate with great behavioral leadership and tolerance. I also believe there was a tremendous amount of resistance, negative chatter, and toxic behavior regarding his decision that night in 1776. The soldiers, the citizens, must have thought, *What is this man doing? Running? Is he a coward? What kind of message is this sending? We're all doomed!*

This is another lesson to be learned: even when you have the Courage to Take Action Relevant to Everyone, you must also have the courage to accept the risk and pay the price.

Courage is the key. You must know your limits as to what action you can take. How do you measure the relevance to others? What's in it for you? Are *you* relevant?

C.A.R.E.—Courage to Take Action Relevant to Everyonee

When I first attempted this assessment for myself, I was humbled. However, with each lacking attribute, there comes opportunity to recruit, opportunity to raise the bar. This has allowed me to enhance my relevance and remain loyal to my company.

Answer the questions and then analyze the response. For example, if you're a tenured employee, break that down: do you really have twenty years of experience? Or is it more like one year twenty times, or maybe five years four times? No answer is right or wrong, but each speaks to things like staleness, reinventing yourself, and subject-matter expertise.

This book now becomes a workbook. Write your analysis here and refer to it, prove its accuracy, and validate the ways to improve as time goes on and you begin to deliver.

C.A.R.E. Skills Assessment:

C.A.R.E. efficiency in the workplace must be honestly assessed, factored into project estimates and discussed at length during employee evaluations. When the company understands that cost, overhead and delivery time is directly associated with C.A.R.E. efficiency, maybe then we'll see C.A.R.E. certification in the workplace established as a requirement.

Category 1: Wisdom (Sam Adams)

1. I'm considered wise in the workplace. This wisdom acquired from lessons learned throughout my career, enhances my relevance beyond my job description and is recognized by my co-workers, peers and superiors.

>   Strongly agree
>   Agree
>   Slightly agree
>   No opinion
>   Slightly disagree
>   Disagree
>   Strongly disagree
>   Not applicable

Why?

How?

Example(s):

C.A.R.E.—Courage to Take Action Relevant to Everyonee

Ways to improve:

2. I'm often asked for my opinion in the workplace about work.

>   Strongly agree
>   Agree
>   Slightly agree
>   No opinion
>   Slightly disagree
>   Disagree
>   Strongly disagree
>   Not applicable

Why?

How?

Example(s):

C.A.R.E.—Courage to Take Action Relevant to Everyonee

Ways to improve:

3. When C.A.R.E. is the motive, teamwork and leadership become one and the same.

    Strongly agree
    Agree
    Slightly agree
    No opinion
    Slightly disagree
    Disagree
    Strongly disagree
    Not applicable

Why?

How?

Example(s):

C.A.R.E.—Courage to Take Action Relevant to Everyonee

Ways to improve:

4. I have the courage to address "issues behind the issues" even if it means project delay.

    Strongly agree
    Agree
    Slightly agree
    No opinion
    Slightly disagree
    Disagree
    Strongly disagree
    Not applicable

Why?

How?

Example(s):

C.A.R.E.—Courage to Take Action Relevant to Everyonee

Ways to improve:

5. I have the courage to step up and say, "We're not where we should be."

> Strongly agree
> Agree
> Slightly agree
> No opinion
> Slightly disagree
> Disagree
> Strongly disagree
> Not applicable

Why?

How?

Example(s):

Ways to improve:

6. My teammates, co-workers and superiors would agree with my assessment ratings for this category.

Strongly agree
Agree
Slightly agree
No opinion
Slightly disagree
Disagree
Strongly disagree
Not applicable

Why?

How?

Example(s);

Ways to improve:

Category 2: Networking (Paul Revere)

1. I'm considered likeable and social in the workplace

    Strongly agree
    Agree
    Slightly agree
    No opinion
    Slightly disagree
    Disagree
    Strongly disagree
    Not applicable

Why?

How?

Example(s):

C.A.R.E.—Courage to Take Action Relevant to Everyonee

Ways to improve:

2. I'm considered an enabler of interaction among my co-workers, including my superiors.

    Strongly agree
    Agree
    Slightly agree
    No opinion
    Slightly disagree
    Disagree
    Strongly disagree
    Not applicable

Why?

How?

Example(s):

C.A.R.E.—Courage to Take Action Relevant to Everyonee

Ways to improve:

3. I freely share all my knowledge, lessons learned and insight specific to the workplace.

> Strongly agree
> Agree
> Slightly agree
> No opinion
> Slightly disagree
> Disagree
> Strongly disagree
> Not applicable

Why?

How?

Example(s):

C.A.R.E.—Courage to Take Action Relevant to Everyonee

Ways to improve:

4. I believe I can make a difference in my company, even by acting alone.

>   Strongly agree
>   Agree
>   Slightly agree
>   No opinion
>   Slightly disagree
>   Disagree
>   Strongly disagree
>   Not applicable

Why?

How?

Example(s):

C.A.R.E.—Courage to Take Action Relevant to Everyonee

Ways to improve:

5. I'm aware of my infra-structure, organization, customers and overall goals and direction of my company.

>   Strongly agree
>   Agree
>   Slightly agree
>   No opinion
>   Slightly disagree
>   Disagree
>   Strongly disagree
>   Not applicable

Why?

How?

Example(s):

C.A.R.E.—Courage to Take Action Relevant to Everyonee

Ways to improve:

6. My teammates, co-workers and superiors would agree with my assessment ratings for this category.

> Strongly agree
> Agree
> Slightly agree
> No opinion
> Slightly disagree
> Disagree
> Strongly disagree
> Not applicable

Why?

How?

Example(s):

Ways to improve:

Category 3: Communication (Thomas Paine)

1. I get to the point quickly and I'm accountable for everything I say. It could be a question, an answer, an opinion, a concern or a suggestion. Whatever point I'm making, I make it as brief and to the point as possible.

Strongly agree
Agree
Slightly agree
No opinion
Slightly disagree
Disagree
Strongly disagree
Not applicable

Why?

How?

Example(s):

C.A.R.E.—Courage to Take Action Relevant to Everyonee

Ways to improve:

2. I do not use the "reply all" feature when using email, unless the reply is relevant to everyone in the chain. I'm accountable to make that judgement prior to sending the reply.

> Strongly agree
> Agree
> Slightly agree
> No opinion
> Slightly disagree
> Disagree
> Strongly disagree
> Not applicable

Why?

How?

Example(s):

Ways to improve:

3. I know the difference between a status and a story.

In a recent meeting at my company, a subject matter expert was reporting status on a critical project. After ten minutes of details, the leader of the meeting finally asked, "are we behind schedule, on schedule or ahead of schedule"?

Strongly agree
Agree
Slightly agree
No opinion
Slightly disagree
Disagree
Strongly disagree
Not applicable

Why?

How?

Example(s):

C.A.R.E.—Courage to Take Action Relevant to Everyonee

Ways to improve:

4. I'm often the one chosen to send out a communication.

> Strongly agree
> Agree
> Slightly agree
> No opinion
> Slightly disagree
> Disagree
> Strongly disagree
> Not applicable

Why?

How?

Example(s):

C.A.R.E.—Courage to Take Action Relevant to Everyonee

Ways to improve:

5. My communications also motivate my team.

>Strongly agree
>Agree
>Slightly agree
>No opinion
>Slightly disagree
>Disagree
>Strongly disagree
>Not applicable

Why?

How?

Example(s):

Ways to improve:

6. My teammates, co-workers and superiors would agree with my assessment ratings for this category.

>   Strongly agree
>   Agree
>   Slightly agree
>   No opinion
>   Slightly disagree
>   Disagree
>   Strongly disagree
>   Not applicable

Why?

How?

Example(s):

C.A.R.E.—Courage to Take Action Relevant to Everyonee

Ways to improve:

Category 4: Commitment (Patrick Henry)

1. I speak in questions.

>   Strongly agree
>   Agree
>   Slightly agree
>   No opinion
>   Slightly disagree
>   Disagree
>   Strongly disagree
>   Not applicable

Why?

How?

Example(s):

C.A.R.E.—Courage to Take Action Relevant to Everyonee

Ways to improve:

2. I convey the passion of commitment in my communications.

   Strongly agree
   Agree
   Slightly agree
   No opinion
   Slightly disagree
   Disagree
   Strongly disagree
   Not applicable

Why?

How?

Example(s):

C.A.R.E.—Courage to Take Action Relevant to Everyonee

Ways to improve:

3. I don't say yes to every task assigned, even if it's a command decision. I always qualify, question and prioritize first.

> Strongly agree
> Agree
> Slightly agree
> No opinion
> Slightly disagree
> Disagree
> Strongly disagree
> Not applicable

Why?

How?

Example(s):

C.A.R.E.—Courage to Take Action Relevant to Everyonee

Ways to improve:

4. Developing "soft skill" expertise will deliver cost efficient results for your company and does not mean you are soft.

    Strongly agree
    Agree
    Slightly agree
    No opinion
    Slightly disagree
    Disagree
    Strongly disagree
    Not applicable

Why?

How?

Example(s):

C.A.R.E.—Courage to Take Action Relevant to Everyonee

Ways to improve:

5. If (or when) I present an idea to my teammates, co-workers or superiors, I only accept rejection provided I left no stone un turned when presenting the idea in the first place.

> Strongly agree
> Agree
> Slightly agree
> No opinion
> Slightly disagree
> Disagree
> Strongly disagree
> Not applicable

Why?

How?

Example(s):

C.A.R.E.—Courage to Take Action Relevant to Everyonee

Ways to improve:

6. My teammates, co-workers and superiors would agree with my assessment ratings for this category.

    Strongly agree
    Agree
    Slightly agree
    No opinion
    Slightly disagree
    Disagree
    Strongly disagree
    Not applicable

Why?

How?

Example(s):

C.A.R.E.—Courage to Take Action Relevant to Everyonee

Ways to improve:

Category 5:
Behavioral leadership (George Washington)

1. I observe before I act.

   Strongly agree
   Agree
   Slightly agree
   No opinion
   Slightly disagree
   Disagree
   Strongly disagree
   Not applicable

Why?

How?

Example(s):

Ways to improve:

2. I'm my harshest critic and I'm 100% accountable for my results in the workplace.

> Strongly agree
> Agree
> Slightly agree
> No opinion
> Slightly disagree
> Disagree
> Strongly disagree
> Not applicable

Why?

How?

Example(s):

C.A.R.E.—Courage to Take Action Relevant to Everyonee

Ways to improve:

3. I'm as close to the actual work as I can be.

>   Strongly agree
>   Agree
>   Slightly agree
>   No opinion
>   Slightly disagree
>   Disagree
>   Strongly disagree
>   Not applicable

Why?

How?

Example(s):

C.A.R.E.—Courage to Take Action Relevant to Everyonee

Ways to improve:

4. I demonstrate behavioral leadership in the workplace.

>   Strongly agree
>   Agree
>   Slightly agree
>   No opinion
>   Slightly disagree
>   Disagree
>   Strongly disagree
>   Not applicable

Why?

How?

Example(s):

Ways to improve:

5. I believe in my strategies but am willing to change them when needed.

>   Strongly agree
>   Agree
>   Slightly agree
>   No opinion
>   Slightly disagree
>   Disagree
>   Strongly disagree
>   Not applicable

Why?

How?

Example(s):

C.A.R.E.—Courage to Take Action Relevant to Everyonee

Ways to improve:

6. My teammates, co-workers and superiors would agree with my assessment ratings for this category.

> Strongly agree
> Agree
> Slightly agree
> No opinion
> Slightly disagree
> Disagree
> Strongly disagree
> Not applicable

Why?

How?

Example(s):

C.A.R.E.—Courage to Take Action Relevant to Everyonee

Ways to improve:

Category 6: C.A.R.E.

1. C.A.R.E. is my motive in the workplace; to have the courage to take action relevant to everyone..

> Strongly agree
> Agree
> Slightly agree
> No opinion
> Slightly disagree
> Disagree
> Strongly disagree
> Not applicable

Why?

How?

Example(s):

Ways to improve:

2. My relevance at work goes beyond my job description.

    Strongly agree
    Agree
    Slightly agree
    No opinion
    Slightly disagree
    Disagree
    Strongly disagree
    Not applicable

Why?

How?

Example(s):

C.A.R.E.—Courage to Take Action Relevant to Everyonee

Ways to improve:

3. C.A.R.E. efficiency is factored into my project estimates.

    Strongly agree
    Agree
    Slightly agree
    No opinion
    Slightly disagree
    Disagree
    Strongly disagree
    Not applicable

Why?

How?

Example(s):

C.A.R.E.—Courage to Take Action Relevant to Everyonee

Ways to improve:

4. C.A.R.E. is discussed at length during my performance assessment.

    Strongly agree
    Agree
    Slightly agree
    No opinion
    Slightly disagree
    Disagree
    Strongly disagree
    Not applicable

Why?

How?

Example(s):

C.A.R.E.—Courage to Take Action Relevant to Everyonee

Ways to improve:

5. I believe the bar can be raised on my performance in the workplace.

> Strongly agree
> Agree
> Slightly agree
> No opinion
> Slightly disagree
> Disagree
> Strongly disagree
> Not applicable

Why?

How?

Example(s):

C.A.R.E.—Courage to Take Action Relevant to Everyonee

Ways to improve:

6. My teammates, co-workers and superiors would agree with my assessment ratings for this category.

>   Strongly agree
>   Agree
>   Slightly agree
>   No opinion
>   Slightly disagree
>   Disagree
>   Strongly disagree
>   Not applicable

Why?

How?

Example(s):

C.A.R.E.—Courage to Take Action Relevant to Everyonee

Ways to improve:

There are eight possible answers for each question. The breakdown is as follows:

Answer	Point Value
Strongly agree	8
Agree	6
Slightly agree	2
No opinion	-5
Slightly disagree	-2
Disagree	-6
Strongly disagree	-8
Not applicable	0

The highest score possible is 288. If you score that high, you're running at 100 percent efficiency with regards to C.A.R.E.

What was your (honest) score? Do the math; what is your efficiency percentage? The difference between your efficiency percentage and full efficiency is your opportunity.

If your C.A.R.E. efficiency is 75 percent, you MUST add 25 percent to your project estimates. Consider this the C.A.R.E. factor.

Imagine that: a soft skill being converted into a metric!

Also—did you select "no opinion" anywhere? Hopefully not! How can you think your job is relevant if you have no opinion?

Now that you know where you are regarding the C.A.R.E efficiency assessment, you must go one step further. Give the assessment to all your team members, and see where they stand. This will help them, and you, progress toward C.A.R.E. certification.

C.A.R.E.—Courage to Take Action Relevant to Everyonee

We must validate question six from each category in the assessment:

My teammates, co-workers and superiors would agree with my assessment ratings for this category.

Question six in each category does NOT mean your teammates have the same answers as you. It means when your teammates read your answers, they would agree they came from you. One of my early corporate teachers, Lem Jones used to say, "what's clear to me is clear to me". Validating question six will either prove this right or wrong.

Do you have the courage to share your assessments with teammates, co workers and even superiors?

There's no personal agenda here, just a quest to assess C.A.R.E. efficiency in your day-to-day workplace environment.

Let's recap. You established the motive of C.A.R.E. You have mentors who also share the same common motive. You've assessed your skills specific to C.A.R.E and specific to the skills your mentors bring to the table.

You've come a long way! If you have the willingness to share your assessments, you've really come a long way!

Twenty Ways to Become C.A.R.E.-Certified

1. *Work each day as if the entire performance will be shown on the evening news.* Back in the '80s, I was a technology consultant for National Community Bank of New Jersey. What was interesting about this bank was they were 100 percent invested only in New Jersey. At year end, the president of the bank would walk around to each employee; their gift was a holiday handshake and one week's gross pay in cash. This was considered a gift, not a bonus.

When he came to my desk, he asked my name while checking through his list. I told him I was a consultant. He said, "Well then, happy holidays."

Since I had the bank president speaking to me at my desk (even if only thirty seconds), I had to make the best of it. I asked, "Can you provide some presidential wisdom that can improve my life?"

He immediately responded, "Sure. Work each day as if the entire performance will be shown on the evening news." It took me a while to digest this, but I get it and I agree.

2. *Always be humble.* Never lead with confidence! Or is it ignorance? Or is it arrogance? I'm never really sure so I leave confidence off the table. I learned this in the '70s! While working for SwissRe insurance, I attended project management training. I had the luxury of learning from the wisdom of Lem Jones, the instructor and employee of IBM's Systems Science Institute.

Lem was an old-timer. He taught me early on about confidence (or is it ignorance, or arrogance?). He told me that in 1902, the British Parliament wanted to eliminate the British patent department in an effort to cut costs. Since it was 1902, the British Parliament was confident everything that could possibly be invented already was!

I remember thinking that if leaders in title could be so wrong in judgment back then, the same could be true today.

Lem possessed two great attributes: motivation and communication. Everything he taught—project management, leadership, teamwork—always came down to those two things. Lem created by following the mantra, *Think opposite!* Be unique. Over the years, this has allowed me to reinvent myself over and over. Thirty-five years later, I'm still surviving and thriving in the ever-changing workplace by thinking opposite; after all, C.A.R.E. is the antithesis of toxic behavior!

Lem Jones also taught me how to be a skillful observer.

I'll never forget my first day on my first consulting assignment in 1980 for Citibank. The person sitting next to me was a seasoned, confident consultant.

"Don't be so nervous," he said, "this assignment is easy. I've been here three weeks and not really doing much." I remember thinking he seemed so confident. I was intimidated, maybe even out of my league.

He was gone by 9:30. No notice.

Wow!

I thought of *The Wizard of Oz*, when Dorothy said, "People come and go so quickly around here."

From that day on, I kept my confidence off the table and my car keys in my pocket, and I learned to work with a sense of urgency.

Confidence has confused me to the point I'm not sure if it's confidence, arrogance, or ignorance. Therefore, to be safe, I leave it off the table completely.

The same can be said of one's personal agenda. In the workplace, one's personal agenda must only be geared toward the common good of the company. If we can't understand that, if we're unsure, we should leave it off the table completely!

3. *Proceed with a sense of urgency.* From that first day on my first consulting assignment, I learned to proceed with a sense of urgency. Even when I was coaching fast-pitch softball, regardless of the score, we played as if we were up by only one run. This was our rule. This attitude keeps you in the zone; it will keep you focused on your task. If, after questioning a task until you're blue in the face, you are still unable to change the direction and must then execute it, do it with a sense of urgency. This is especially true with command decisions from above. Regardless of the outcome, a sense of urgency will bring the task to fruition sooner. The risk is less.

4. *Recruit a diverse skill set.* The technology field has always been diverse in terms of available skill sets. Is there a communicator on your team? A speaker? Someone who will network with other organizations? Recruit based on the opportunities presented from the above skills assessment, but only recruit those who share the

common motive. For me, the objective is to recruit a diverse set of skills with a common motive; not a "team of rivals," but teammates who all believe in C.A.R.E.

In 1992, right around the time of the Gulf War, I was in the middle of an entrepreneurial venture: the fifteen-minute job search for technologists. We take job searching for granted now, but back then, this was groundbreaking. During the development, I recruited what I thought was a diverse skill set that included; marketing experts, skilled technicians and a banker with a technology background... I thought I had it all. I was missing the common motive, though; nobody cared. On top of that, I couldn't (or didn't) sell it. Everyone went in his or her own direction, and in the end, the project self destructed.

However, great things are possible when teammates all believe in C.A.R.E.

In 2003 back at Citigroup, I was running around in a corporate chaotic stupor when a new consultant asked me what I needed. I stopped in my tracks and said, "A teammate." Eva was the most efficient teammate I ever worked with. Why? Because she shared the same common motive; she cared. C.A.R.E. is in her behavior. Eva is C.A.R.E.-certified. Together, we achieved great results. I even received a reward from the company as a top performer!

5. *Maintain your watch list.* This is my most effective working tool. Status reports have become meaningless, with too much detail and too many questions left unanswered: when, why, how. However, a watch list only speaks to issues and concerns that may cause a date to be missed. I've since tailored my watch list to include the C.A.R.E. efficiency rating for each project. The lower the rating, the higher the concern. I break it down into two

parts: first, the actual issues and concerns divided by my various functions; and second, the metrics.

Prior to this writing, I was sour on metric reporting and micromanaging. Today's workplace is a politically correct environment where everything is measured by metrics to the point of too much monitoring. Why? Using metrics so extensively promotes distrust; it completely changes the emotion from care to fear. There's too much monitoring in the workplace, too many speed bumps. Receive desktop support? Upon completion we get a survey. All hands meeting? Survey. Company event? Another survey. Third party performance assessment? Another survey. Fail to respond? We receive a second notice. These surveys monitor the responses at the individual employee level. This forces us all to participate, yes, but we generally react in a negative manner: What is the purpose? What are the benefits? What becomes of these surveys? We question excessive workload—or, maybe excessive is not the proper word. Maybe it should be *unnecessary* workload.

One former superior of mine (only one!) did speak up and provide, input around metrics and micromanaging. He said, "In my opinion, the level of oversight and metrics is somewhat directly proportionate to the maturity level of an organization.

"Sometime the level of 'micromanagement' might seem extreme, but until an organization becomes functional, a strong management team is required to move the organization. One could argue that sometimes management itself is dysfunctional and is the cause for the immaturity in the organization, and in those cases, I would agree the masses have to work to chart a course to maturity."

This point is well taken. Organizations in the workplace are constantly being reorganized, outsourced, and downsized. The maturity is always in question. I have since reevaluated the role of metrics and micromanaging. I utilize my watch list to not only watch, but also to monitor.

6. *Begin to deliver.* Begin the day-to-day process of utilizing C.A.R.E. as your motive, maintaining the watch list, and communicating accordingly. Every interaction is an opportunity. This is your new behavior in the workplace. Start recruiting. Know your chain of command; respect it, but don't hesitate to ask questions. Rome wasn't built in a day, but on day one there was some construction! So start constructing! Start by preparing your watch list.

7. *Question everything.* Why is this priority? What is the impact if not delivered? What if I can't commit? Who will develop the test scripts? Be relentless with your questioning. Act as if you're the only one on the project. Have you noticed the number of questions asked in this book?

Back to our visionary and another vision. This corporate visionary determined the best way to raise the performance bar among the workforce was to implement a Top Ten/Bottom Ten program. Every month the workforce was ranked within their respective groups. Once coached, the bottom ten would, it was hoped, work their way up the line.

At face value, it was a good thing. Those in the top ten would get recognized, bottom ten would be coached to step up and become top ten. The net result was that the bar was raised. However, the different lines of business leaders applied their personal agendas, turning this into a dangerous weapon, a bad thing which led to the demise of many—including the program.

This program was utilized to "move out" the bottom ten. Metrics were kept and shared at review time. There were some

C.A.R.E.—Courage to Take Action Relevant to Everyonee

groups with only two or three people. Every month they were ranked. Imagine having two people in your group, and every month, one had to be top ten, the other bottom ten. Co workers A and B both had recent deliverables. However, Co-worker A's deliverable was flawed; it caused production failure that put customers at risk. These problems were addressed in a cold-sweat panic in the middle of the night; they were resolved, and so A entered the top ten. Co-worker B also had a deliverable, but his was not flawed. Everything was working as delivered, the requirements were met. Co-worker B was bottom ten because he was quietly working on his next deliverable. He was under the radar; there were no recent metrics of accomplishment. While I won't say A should've been bottom ten, I will say B should *not* have been.

This program was a nightmare, pitting co-worker against co-worker. The politically connected always landed in the top ten, while the others seemed to consistently be bottom ten. What exactly does bottom ten mean? Was it measured against the common good of the company? The personal agenda of the immediate supervisor? What becomes of the majority who remain under the radar, the eighty percent? How many bottom ten were actually coached out of that ranking? Who developed the coaching?

This created a lack of trust which, when broken, can never be repaired. There is suffering to this day, all because competition was taken beyond face value into personal agenda territory, where it self destructed.

I understand the difference between command and consensus. I understand that my job is to determine *how* a command is to be implemented, not why. Still, that's no reason to avoid dialogue through questions. You can always question why just to be clear on the task, and you can certainly ask as many questions as needed to deliver effectively.

We need to be more accountable upward with our questions. This will happen when we become C.A.R.E.-certified.

8. *Be a teammate.* On Mickey Mantle's monument in Yankee Stadium, it reads, "A Great Teammate." That is the highest compliment one can receive in the workplace!

Teams in the corporate workplace are common. But are they real teams? Teams of equal parts? Teams of ordinary people collaborating to achieve extraordinary results? Or are they groups of people being assigned tasks by a leader? Are they really only "teams of personal agenda"?

Rarely have I come across a team that wasn't metric managed, monitored and therefore suppressed of any opportunity to create or take risks. Both are essential to deliver the results of which we must be willing to be held accountable for.

I was leading a seminar during the summer of 2008 in Pasadena. I was speaking about teamwork, teammates, and teams. I had an interaction with a small business owner during a seminar workshop session.

He said with confidence (or is it arrogance? or ignorance?), "You don't have to discuss this with me. I'm always preaching teamwork. The meaning of team is, 'Together Everyone Achieves More'!" He went on, "As the leader, I'm always telling my team what I expect from them. I know how to play this game, how to get production out of my resources."

Work is not a game, the workplace is not a playing field, and the workers are not players or resources; they're people, with hearts, souls, and brains.

C.A.R.E.—Courage to Take Action Relevant to Everyonee

This is a case of a leader implementing his personal agenda! This team is really executing tasks specific to what the leader is dictating. This is not a team.

The small business owner represents a leader in title only. This leader in title is giving zero credibility to his team. It is unnecessary to form external expectations about a true team. The expectation is in the title: teamwork. Once a leader takes ownership, it's no longer a team.

I see this over and over in the workplace today. We're included in a team, only to be metric-managed and limited to the personal agenda of the leader. Teams need room to breathe in order to succeed!

9. *Teamwork.* As individuals on a team, we are accountable for our deliverables, and accountable for the success of the team. We should assess the skill set of the group and leverage accordingly.

When we think of George Washington, we think of a leader. I think of him as a teammate. His leadership was in his behavior first, which only later came in title. Washington specifically refused the title of "king" when it was offered him; he knew that the last thing the American people needed was a return to the hierarchy they had just rebelled against. He wanted a collaborative government; he led through teamwork.

10. *Be a leader through your behavior.* When Sam Adams felt it was time to assemble a group to discuss the plan for liberation from England's tyranny, he was showing behavioral leadership. When Patrick Henry stepped up and drove home the importance of liberty, he was being a leader. When Thomas Paine, an Englishman, informed the American public that they

were ordinary people capable of extraordinary things, he too was leading.

Leadership is not about a title, but about behavior. Leadership must be embedded in your day-to-day workplace activities, in your very heartbeat.

Where leadership gets complicated is in the price.

I go back to my fast-pitch coaching days for this lesson. Baseball has always been my passion, but since I have two daughters, little league meant softball. Fast-pitch softball became my new passion. For ten years I was a Junior Olympic fast-pitch softball coach.

After spending too much time critiquing and blaming the various fast-pitch organizations and programs, I decided to form my own. Eventually, there were four teams, for the different age groups (twelve and under, fourteen, sixteen and eighteen). Each team had approximately fifteen players. Once you've multiplied by two parents and added some other coaches, you have an organization of approximately 190 people.

The price I paid for this decision was enormous. I was determined to make this organization successful no matter what; that was my personal agenda. If a player couldn't pay the fee, I paid it; if the cost for travel to a national tournament was too high for a player or family, I paid it. I addressed all player problems; if a team was struggling, I brought in paid coaches. I was so close to the people in the organization, I lost sight of everything. I became associated with every problem. My life was chaos, my family life in ruin. Parents never acknowledged I was paying this price, as they were working on their own personal agendas to get their daughters some recognition. There were times I was working through the night at work on a bank acquisition, only to finish up 8:00 am, which left just enough time to drive in a panic from

Manhattan to upstate New York in order to get to the meeting place by 9:00, and lead the parents and players to our weekend tournament.

All the while, although I couldn't see it, the players were unbiased and loyal to each other. They were close and attended each others' needs—injuries, hunger, emotional support, whatever was needed. They were willing to move mountains, and did just that many times.

Great examples of teamwork come out regardless of the personal agendas of the leaders, provided the motive is care. The players all cared for each other. One time at a state tournament in upstate New York, my team (aged twelve and under) was waiting to play their second game. These tournaments are brutal, double-elimination sets; you lose twice and you go home. The first game is crucial. We had won our first game, so we were now in the winner's bracket. Parents were strutting around while the players tried to prepare for the second game. Unfortunately due to rain, the second game was delayed. Because of the remaining games and the need to complete the entire tournament by the next day, we had to play at 2:00 am. This was a twelve-year-old team!

Since I was the leader, I had to decide if we should play or not. We could have easily gone back to the hotel with a forfeit and still have had the opportunity to play at least one game the next day. This (at least) justified the hotel costs.

The parents, though, wanted blood. Many wanted to leave, while many others were holding me accountable for staying and trying to win. Come midnight, I took the team aside, even waking those who were sleeping, to discuss the situation. "If we play and lose," I said, "we'll remember it for the rest of our lives. Is this what we want?"

My team looked at me like I was not equal to the title of coach. To them, there was no question: we would play this game. They believed in themselves, in me. They were leading me. When the motive is care, teamwork and leadership are one and the same.

The girls won the game. Their performance was brilliant. They executed as a team, providing a priceless example of when C.A.R.E. is the motive, teamwork and leadership become one and the same. We got back to the hotel at 4:30 in the morning, asking for a wake up at 8:00 for our next game. At the age of twelve!

I will remember them all for the rest of my life.

What about the lesson in price? Many parents went to the newspapers to complain. They looked at this as a selfish act on my part, with no concern for the team or the parents. One parent in particular, whose daughter just couldn't stay awake and therefore didn't even sit with the team, complained of abusive conditions. Along with that, during the game I utilized a pinch runner in an attempt to score a run. The parent of that player became livid since his daughter would not be playing the whole game. He became so angry that he withdrew his daughter from the team and started an organization based on his personal agenda.

Many of the other parents by habit sided with the most aggressive. Our greatest moment as a team was diminished to confrontation. The team was never the same.

I was unprepared for this price, and therefore not able to defend, persuade, or inspire. I just paid it.

There will always be a price. Leadership in title can be at times too costly to bear. That's why there are so few leaders.

We have to be willing to pay the price of leadership in order to lead. This team was a team of ordinary players achieving extraordinary results. This example of teamwork is priceless! The price that was paid was because of my personal agenda.

C.A.R.E.—*Courage to Take Action Relevant to Everyonee*

I will always respect leaders in title, having walked a mile in their shoes. Leaders in title need to stay focused on the big picture, and trust their teams to deliver.

11. *You don't have to be a leader in title to lead.* In 1995, I was part of a conversion team for Alltel during a bank merger. This was the first time I was working for that company as a technology consultant. We worked many stressful hours, but let me fast-forward to the night of the actual conversion, when I was tasked (for some reason) with the final element: making the system available for all the customers. This occurs after all the work is complete, somewhere around 5:00 AM. The task is quick but critical.

I couldn't understand why I was chosen for this. Why me? Did I ask or question? No. Why me, all alone? What if I needed support, what if I had a problem—hell, what if I didn't show up? Did I ask? No.

I did show up. I worked on my conversion tasks during the evening, and when time came for this final implementation, it was only me and tumbleweed.

I remember thinking, *Tonight, my team is me. It's too late for me to worry about why the leaders chose to have this crucial task supported by one person and after that one person has been working round the clock.*

I remember executing my tasks very slowly. I remember running late; I remember the cold sweat; I remember every single breath during that crucial two-hour timeframe. Yet somehow, I completed the tasks; the merged banks were now one. But I was disappointed at the lack of team, especially when the game was on the line.

I bring this up because I was not a leader in title, but I was suddenly leading. I had no mentors back then to provide any guidance. There was no reason for me to be alone that night. But this was my doing, too, since I never questioned anything. I put myself in that position by blaming everyone else. If I knew then what I know now, I certainly would have had a less stressful evening, and there would have been less risk to those two banks on the night of conversion. Nobody had my back that night, and that is unacceptable.

I needed to be like Paul Revere, to network and recruit teammates willing to be there until the end. The company leaders were not promoting C.A.R.E., so nobody was. This makes me angry. This needs to stop. Absence of C.A.R.E.-certified leaders in title doesn't mean absence of C.A.R.E.-certified leaders at the bottom.

Leadership opportunities are plentiful in the workplace today. However, it's difficult to seize them when you're alone. At a prior company, General Adjustment Bureau (GAB), I was working as a newly-appointed application manager. The superior said my new team was held together by Ritchie. "He's been here for years; he's our guy; we go way back. But you need to be careful with everyone else. Watch them carefully, and let me know immediately if any action needs to be taken against them."

Okay, I thought. *Hostile environment; what else is new!*

During the day, the team (minus Ritchie) was running around like crazy trying to keep up with all the problems. Where was Ritchie? Seems he was working nights until things stabilized. The team all toed the line, agreeing, "He's making sure everything runs smoothly at night to ensure the customers even have a system in the morning."

I called Ritchie that night at 2:00 am. He was monitoring the jobs that are running.

"Hmm, so, how long do these jobs run?" I asked.

Ritchie replied, "All night."

"Any issues?"

"Nah. Why?"

Since all the problems were from the results of the nightly process and not due to the failure of the nightly process, I put Ritchie on days and rotated the rest of the team into nightly support. There were three team members, so it was one month of nights, two months of days.

My superior almost fired me on the spot, as he screamed, "Who the hell do you think you are? You can't make shift changes without my permission. What are you trying to prove? I don't want those guys on nights; if they can't cut it on days, we'll cut them."

I told him that was a terrible idea, adding, "Ritchie is of no value; he's working alone at night with no tasks. He's not here during the day to provide any expertise, or to address the root cause of any problem, or to share his knowledge to the others."

"Tough! That's your problem, not Ritchie's. If you don't like it, you can leave too!"

That same day I received a call from a former company to see if I was in the market to come back, which I did. I jumped at this new opportunity because I was not yet C.A.R.E.-certified; I did not have the courage to stay and fight.

I mention all this because, to this day, that failure lives with me. I saw the opportunity, but the environment was too hostile to even listen. I was working alone; the guys on days said or did nothing. They were actually angry with me because I put them on the radar. Ritchie wanted nothing to do with any accountability.

The superior was just outright evil. He once called a meeting at 7:00 AM on December 26th; the morning after Christmas day!

To make a difference in that workplace, I needed help; I needed teammates. There were none. Sometimes, even when given the opportunity to lead, you won't succeed despite having the right solutions. You must first recruit the right team. If this doesn't occur, there should be C.A.R.E. efficiency alerts all over your watch list. I should have presented the idea to the evil supervisor with a third party present prior to implementing any changes, sure, but the conflict arose from the supervisor's paranoia that his personal agenda would no longer be fulfilled.

12. *Communicate effectively.* Early in my career, I was on a call at 3:00 AM. Production was down, root cause undetermined. I was low man on the totem pole and told not to speak on the call.

The leader of the call asked who was on the line?

Everyone spoke at once.

He asked everyone to speak one at a time.

Again everyone spoke at once. I had no idea what was being said. It was as if the conversation was in a different language coming over the phone lines with unbearable static!

Even though I had been told not to speak, I spoke. "Let's start on the West Coast, and move around the country. When you're finished, I have a question, and then you can continue."

Mr. West Coast spoke. I had no idea what he said; something about "small packets"

When he finished, I asked, "What does that mean?"

Total silence! It was clear there were too many hard skilled technicians on the call but no soft skill communicators.

Do you get to the point quickly? Do you even know the point you need to make? You may not be in the position of being a subject-matter expert in your field, but when communicating there's no reason not to be an expert on what you're saying, and saying it for everyone to understand. A subject matter expert (SME) is the most knowledge source of the topic at hand. It could be a project, task or even just communicating in conversation. If you're on a work related call, there's a reason and there must be accountability to speak of the topic at hand and only to the point. If you're on a call and there's no leader, you're the leader!

Can you communicate in the way that best suits the audience? Sometimes it will be email, sometimes phone, and sometimes just plain old-fashioned conversation.

If you're passionate about something, say it! Emails can't express emotion the way conversation can. You can be politically correct with an email recap after the fact.

Earlier I described how corporate might say likeability is not a technical skill. I beg to differ. Do you communicate more easily, more frequently with someone you like?

13. *Likeability too is a good promoter of communication.* All the C.A.R.E. components benefit from likeability, as do my teammates, my superiors, and in fact, my entire company.

You pay a price when ignoring likeability. You're often bypassed or avoided, which leads to being uninformed. If you're being avoided and uninformed, you're not relevant, and therefore not a trusted teammate.

Don't confuse likeability with being soft. I confront, argue, and disagree with the best of them, but I can still be likeable. How? I don't negotiate, wheedle, or demand; I communicate facts in the hopes of persuading others to see my point. Better yet, I inspire! Acting in this manner promotes trust. This is what being C.A.R.E. certified is all about. The people on the other end of the communication trust what they're hearing is sincere.

When I think about communication, I go back to Thomas Paine and Patrick Henry. They both communicated with a sense of urgency, like true leaders must; you could hear the passion in their words. They were rebels with a cause!

Over a half million copies of *Common Sense* were produced; author unknown! How's that for being humble? Yet Thomas Paine knew how to reach an audience. George Washington kept Thomas Paine at his hip, because of this value. They rode the front lines together.

When you communicate, you must reach your audience. However you do this, make sure your message sinks in. Avoid the "reply all" feature on email whenever possible. Put some thought behind your response. No need to send it to the world, just the sender. It shows consideration, sincerity, and care.

You can tell how you're doing in many ways: feedback, questions, and actions taken from your message. Take this to heart. Your communication method will be tweaked accordingly according to the intended audience.

For example: When communicating with a "tough guy," don't be so tough. This will cause immediate confrontation. Your message will be lost; in fact, it will most likely be stomped on!

I've learned that tough guys are really passionate guys in disguise. They're defending their honor for the common good of the company, just like Patrick Henry. Why else would the corporate superiors tolerate the behavior?

So get to the point quickly, explain the benefits, and then have the accountability to be subject-matter expert on the topic you're bringing up.

14. *Earn trust.* In the workplace, "The only thing that matters is the result." But you must remember that results are for the common good of the company, and not at the expense of others.

The best way to establish trust in the workplace is to deliver results.

How can we get there?

Are you relevant at work? Are you a subject-matter expert in your job description? Do you even *know* your job description? Remember your job description is whatever it is that you do on a day-to-day basis.

Based on the results of the C.A.R.E. assessment, find ways in your strength's to promote your relevance. Seize the opportunities to improve upon it.

The point is you must do more than merely complete your job's assigned tasks. You must pursue relevance beyond your assigned task. Execute tasks, and you're a co-worker. Share in the success of a deliverable for the common good of the company, and you're a teammate.

Trust will expedite end-to-end delivery. Projects will cost less. Trust alone will provide cost saves to the company, because every member of the team will know that the group is working toward a common goal.

Trust will bring corporate direction to fruition quickly. This is important to understand. Remember that direction from superiors, visionaries, or other people managers may not be the best approach for the common good of the company. But if the team working on the task has that goal in mind, the company will benefit regardless.

Find your relevance and promote it. Make sure your results are not at the expense of others. Do this, and the trust will come.

A good place to start is with our early project estimates. This is what corporate uses to allocate money for the project. This must be an accurate estimate; it can't be perceived as spin by us to pad the dates per our personal agendas, so we can deliver "early" and exceed expectations. C.A.R.E efficiency must be factored into project estimates.

Be cautious around broken trust. There are two sides; trust can be broken by you, or trust can be broken by others. Either way, it's usually a result of a personal agenda trumping the common good.

When trust is broken by others, I suggest you remain tolerant. Statistics certainly show that the main reason leaders are replaced is broken trust. On the surface, it could be presented as lack of results, using metrics to pass the blame, but eventually, when one leader consistently has metrics that show failure, trust breaks down and that leader will be held accountable.

15. *Establish loyalty.* Loyalty engenders trust. I have had many teammates (including myself) confident in our loyalty only to end up leaving the company when results didn't fit our personal agendas. We need to be loyal always, without our personal agenda figuring into it. Where is the fight in us? Great leaders have come forward during times of controversy and change. We need to bring this out, not crawl back, or leave the company. This is the loyalty the company needs. It must be unbiased!

Preaching loyalty is not the same as being loyal through action. The first is not loyalty. Many times we preach loyalty because we're still here, because it's politically correct.

My company prefers loyalty through action, even if it means supporting decisions I may not agree with, for the common good of the company. If, after presenting my case using my C.A.R.E. assessment and all nine components to persuade, the decision goes somewhere other than the direction I preferred, I still support the task. I could have been wrong, or not persuasive enough. However, by providing unbiased loyalty, the task will come to fruition more quickly, and that is always relevant to the common good of the company.

16. *Network your (new) character.* This character is one to be proud of, especially if you've become C.A.R.E. certified. Now share it, be an example and demonstrate by participation. However I caution about being too confident (or is it ignorant? or arrogant?) Network as a humble teammate. When networking (both inside and outside your immediate team), explain the benefits of factoring C.A.R.E. efficiency into all project estimates and the value of watch list reporting.

17. *Learn tolerance.* Learn to tolerate what you can't control: bonuses for upper seniors who may not be close enough to the actual work as they should, or corporate direction from visionaries that never make anything better, often times leading to their own demise at the expense of the company. Learn not to tolerate what you *can* control: you, your behavior, and your deliverables.

Earlier in this book, I described how corporate today would reject my mentors. Don't think for a minute this didn't occur during their time as well. Those five men showed great tolerance. Politicians trashed their ideas; everything you can think of was thrown at them. In fact, John Adams tried to claim ownership of *Common Sense*. (Remember it was published anonymously.) He felt the pamphlet expressed his principles, so as politicians go, why not take credit? Thomas Paine remained tolerant.

These men still moved forward to raise a nation, leaving no stone unturned to deliver results.

Tolerance has been my biggest self-improvement, my greatest accomplishment. When my company looks past me for participation on issues that speak directly to my mission, I remain tolerant. When co-workers accuse me of "sucking up" for my own personal agenda, I remain tolerant. If (or when) results don't come out as I would have preferred, I remain tolerant. If there is confrontation, I remain tolerant. If I'm not getting involved in the high profile projects, I remain tolerant. Tolerance is in my foundation. This is where it belongs. This is where my mentors would tell me it belongs.

I'm tolerant with what I can't control. An example is the level of off-shoring of work. Offs-shoring is what I call "a fact of life after the fact." By that I mean it's been done, already in place. Outsourcing is no longer a pending concern but part of our business as usual. Since this is a command decision, my questions are focused more around how to make it work.

Unfortunately, the outsourced vendors are in dire need of soft-skill training. They lack big-picture skills, and the ability to communicate passion about a deliverable. Because I'm relentlessly utilizing the C.A.R.E. efficiency assessment to improve on every opportunity, I'm not tolerant of the failure of what I can control—and with outsourcing; it's the recruiting and selection of the personnel. When I recruit, I question very carefully, even if it means project delay. I'm especially careful when the term "specialist" is used. Special in what? It's my job, my accountability to my company, to make sure they're truly special, unique to their role. If that's the case, embrace them. If not, find someone else, even if it means project delay.

The British hired specialists to help them fight in the Revolutionary war, the Hessians. George Washington took them out in one day! One Christmas morning!

Be wary of specialists, and if they're not special, don't tolerate them.

All right, so we have leaned to be tolerant. What does that mean?

Tolerance is not a result, but a holding pattern, a yield sign slowing us down from getting the desired results we're looking to achieve. When I'm tolerant, I proceed with caution.

Maybe the tolerance we're experiencing is toward us; from our superiors, peers and teammates. Maybe our message is not clear; our communication of choice is not getting through. Maybe what we're looking to achieve is ahead of its time. Or maybe its time has passed? What we see as tolerance could in fact be missed opportunity.

Maybe we're just flat-out wrong!

We must be very analytical here. In order to go down the right path, to take the proper action, we have to drill down the what and the why of whatever it is we're tolerating, with the sole purpose of getting it resolved.

I've learned not to tolerate my limitations. I utilize my C.A.R.E. efficiency to improve accordingly.

18. *Leverage every opportunity.* Lessons learned, co-workers' thoughts, peer reviews—everything presents an opportunity for change and excellence. Remember it's not about you becoming a hero; it's about delivering results for the good of the company.

If I hadn't learned the meaning and value of leveraging in the workplace early, my career would have been very short.

Paul Revere and Thomas Paine are great examples of leveraging opportunities to achieve their goals. The famous ride of Paul Revere was no individual act, just the execution of a well-thought-out plan. Without leverage, it would never have happened. From Thomas Paine, we heard for the first time about ordinary people doing extraordinary things, and were motivated to contribute.

Teamwork and trusting others gives us leverage to achieve our goals.

19. *Lead with C.A.R.E.* Care is your motive in the workplace. Care for the common good of the company. Unlimited results can only occur if care is your motive.

Start with your job description; with care as your motive, make it relevant, and make its relevance known to others. Then let others know of this foundation through your actions. Be tolerant. When the time comes to deliver, go back to the earlier mission: to be trusted as a teammate to deliver results for the common good of the company.

20. *Collaborate.* We need to collaborate. Every interaction is an opportunity to share ideas, to discuss the opportunities, to develop the appropriate action plans, to proceed with a sense of urgency. This is teamwork—no metrics, no escalating, just collaboration. No appointments necessary, no meeting agenda needed.

Imagine a workplace where this form of collaboration is commonplace. Imagine a workplace where hallway conversation consists of how to improve delivery. Imagine a workplace where the conversation during lunch is around the testability of a requirement and not critique of the executive board.

Collaboration is not a place for gossip, political spin, or personal agenda. In today's workplace, too much collaboration time is spent complaining about the salaries of our superiors, the level of outsourcing, everything we can pass blame on without having to accept any accountability.

The Wheels of Collaboration

The Opportunity Wheel

Spin it for the opportunity to collaborate on an opportunity.

C.A.R.E.—Courage to Take Action Relevant to Everyonee

The TLC Component Wheel

Spin it to select the component and to collaborate about the opportunity.

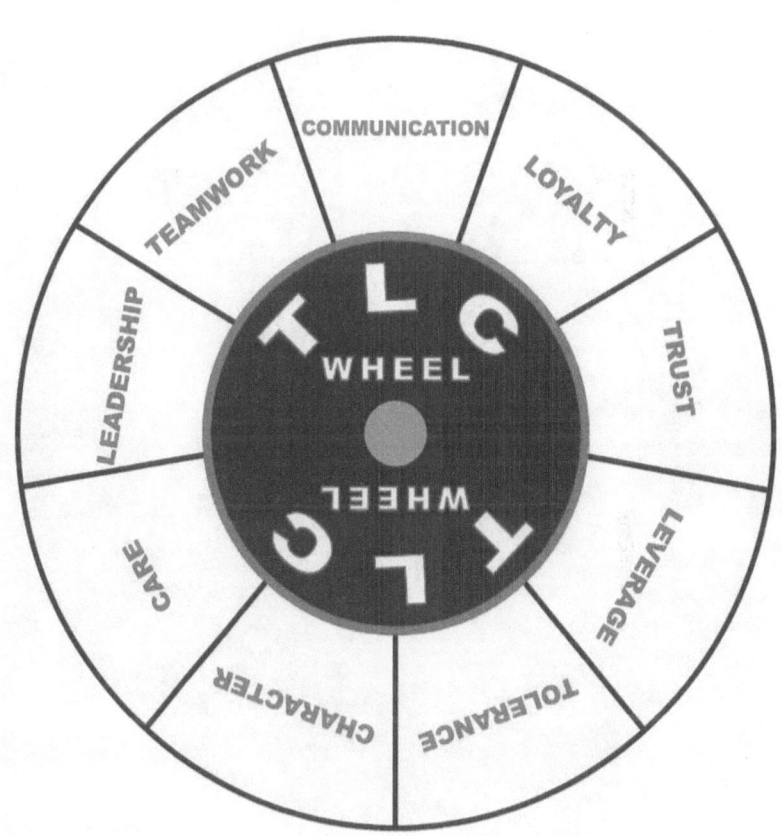

Charles Lobosco

The Mentor Wheel

Spin it to select the mentor and the style of which to work the TLC component to seize the opportunity.

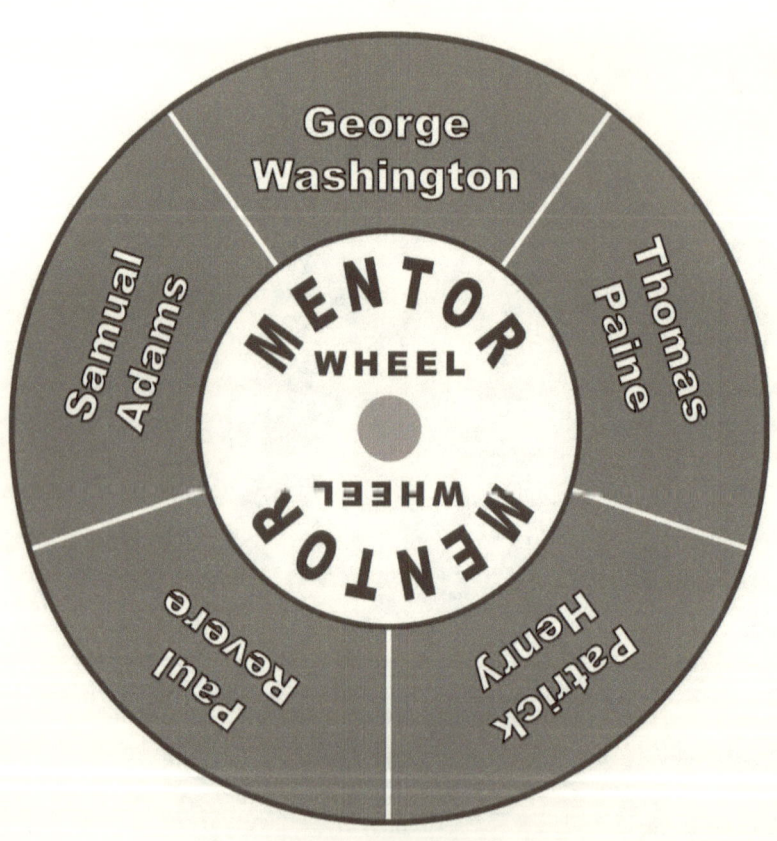

Collaboration

How do we begin the collaboration process? Where do we start? What are the topics of collaboration? Who participates?

We spin the collaboration wheels! This exercise is designed to get the dialogue process started. These wheels are displayed in the workplace. In the lobby, cafeteria, conference rooms. The wheels are "spun" to select the opportunity of the day, the TLC component which drives the conversation and the mentor of which style to use during the collaboration.

Let's spin and apply as an example:

The Opportunity Wheel selects *achieve NOT at the expense of others*.
The TLC component wheel selects *tolerance*
The Mentor wheel selects *Samuel Adams*.

This opportunity is huge. Results must not come at the expense of others. If this occurs (as it often does), the results will be tainted. If you achieve via bullying, the expected results will not hold up.

Tolerance here means you must tolerate the various forms of resistance from others and work through them. Results are not specific to your personal agenda; you can't achieve to satisfy yourself. Results are for the common good of the company.

I referred earlier to Samuel Adams as the father of the forefathers. One of the many attributes he possessed he was that he never demanded recognition for his actions. In today's corporate environment, he would work behind the scenes for the good of the company.

Sam Adams has been around the block long enough to know how to deal with resistance, how to ensure results are achieved, but not at the expense of others. I see him first qualifying the resistance. Is it personal? Political? Then he would do the same for the results. Are the results truly for the common good of the company? If your results don't measure up, be prepared to be accountable. Sam Adams is wise enough to see through the politics, and see the issue at face value. If you come out of your personal agenda, use him as a mentor, you can ensure results achieved are NOT at the expense of others.

Let's spin and apply as another example:

The Opportunity Wheel selects *question everything*.
The TLC component wheel selects *communication*.
The Mentor wheel selects *Patrick Henry*.

Using Patrick Henry as a mentor to question everything is a great way to communicate—in the hallways, the conference rooms, at the water cooler, anywhere. Communication by questioning everything really gets the dialogue going. The below questions are for you to ask yourself.

Do you feel (specific to your actions and performance), the bar can be raised?
Is care your motive?

Do you care about the success of the company, project, and team?

Are you aware acceptance of a task or project is, in effect, a contract to deliver?

Are you aware any persuasion needs to be done before the acceptance?

Do you accept every task assigned?

If this was your own business, and the money was coming out of your pocket, would you pay someone the same salary as you're getting today to do the same job and get the same performance?

Are you honest with yourself?

Do you think you can do a better job than your immediate supervisor, any other superior, any teammate or co-worker?

Do you know your current job description?

Does your job description match what you do?

Would you be happy if your workday was presented in full on the evening news unknown to you?

Do you know the current organizational chart of your group and/or the company?

Have you shared anything positive about the job or company with anyone at work?

If you lost your job, would you blame someone else?

If you're late or miss a deliverable, do you blame someone else?

Do you tolerate office politics?

Have you ever made a decision that was not in the majority?

Are you a go to person at work for critical deliverables?

Are you a big-picture person?

Do you know your infrastructure?

Would your teammates agree with your answers?

Would you mind if they shared your answers, without you present?

Do you support group deliverables you don't agree with?

Given the opportunity to address your group as a superior, would you make a difference?

Do you have ideas, visions, and suggestions to improve your area at work?

Are you technically proficient with every aspect of your job?

Do you leverage help and/or assistance when needed?

Are you guilty of hitting "reply all" too much?

Are you tolerant?

I've used the collaboration wheels to really hone in on self assessment. When I replay my day and see something that needs improvement, I immediately turn to the collaboration wheels to determine; what would Patrick Henry say? How would George Washington develop a strategy to resolve this? What wisdom would Samuel Adams provide to give me a better understanding of the underlying cause?

This tool works! It brought me out of denial, keeps me grounded and provides insight that gives me the courage to stay and fight. Spinning the collaboration wheels helped me become C.A.R.E. certified.

Conclusion

For the record, my five mentors all lived long lives. They were able to see the fruits of their labor. I hope to be able to do the same, to live long and see the fruits of mine.

My current company has treated me well and I intend to stay and fight. Much has changed since I've been on the wagon to sunset my personal agenda. I can say there is no corporate conspiracy. I can say C.A.R.E. is well received by the company, my teammates, the shareholders, and the customers. My job is relevant! My company needs me now more than ever. My mission statement supports their need.

I'm grateful for all the people I've met, and for the opportunity to share in their success.

We need to trust that right is right. Going forward, where we go as a workforce all depends on our ability to act upon the takeaways from this book. We must ensure to utilize the two tools provided to develop and maintain C.A.R.E. certification; the C.A.R.E. efficiency assessment and the collaboration wheels. We must make C.A.R.E. our motive in the workplace.

C.A.R.E. certification in the workplace means commitment to the mission statement:

<u>To be trusted as a teammate to deliver results for the common good of the company and not at the expense of others.</u>

And commitment to:
1. Revisit the C.A.R.E. Efficiency Assessment on a regular basis
2. Sunset your personal agenda in the workplace
3. Proceed with a sense of urgency and a willingness to be influenced
4. Lead from the bottom

I am a modern-day Paul Revere. I am recruiting, looking to the workforce to rise up, be accountable, to care, and to make a difference.

Action needs to begin somewhere. It starts with "I," and then becomes "we." Then we're a team; a team of ordinary people doing extraordinary things.

And then the bar will be raised!

About the Author

Charles A. Lobosco, CSL

"Experience in the face of adversity is better than learning from a university"

Charlie Lobosco is a Certified Seminar Leader, Corporate Technology Executive, Coach and Teammate. Charlie has spent over thirty five years in corporate as a consultant and VP executive for Fortune 100 and Fortune 500 companies. Charlie speaks with a unique sense of urgency and call for immediate action. C.A.R.E. – building a better workplace starts with you! reflects his enthusiasm and passion in a way only he can present.

For inquiries: www.charliespeaking.com

Author's Career

While I'll say I really regret not climbing the corporate ladder for one company, I'll say it is the current practice. I'll also say the diverse exposure to ALL the companies I've been a part of has been priceless!

1973–present

AIG, Alltel, Chemical bank, Chase, Citigroup, Excel Plastics, General Adjustment Bureau, JPM Chase, Kobrand, Lever Brothers, Medco, Merrill Lynch, MHT Bank, Minolta, Monroe Group, National Community Bank, Prudential, Republic National Bank, Security Pacific Bank, Standard Motor Products, Systematics, Swissre, Ward Foods, Zwicker Electric

BECOME C.A.R.E.-CERTIFIED!

When you're C.A.R.E.-certified, you receive a C.A.R.E. pin. Wear it! It will draw teammates to you. The pin means you have the fight of Patrick Henry, the wisdom of Sam Adams, the ability to communicate like Thomas Paine, the behavioral leadership of George Washington, and the endless ability to network, to leave no stone unturned in your quest to deliver, like Paul Revere. You are relevant. You have the Courage to take Action Relevant to Everyone! We need to see the workplace flooded with C.A.R.E. pins.

Plan to attend a seminar! Contact me for details:
Email charlie@charliespeaking.com
1-800-801-1886
www.charliespeaking.com

"The only way to establish trust in the workplace is to deliver results"

Thank you!

If you've read this book with a willingness to be influenced and participated in the assessments, I say thank you!

Thank you and all the best!

Charlie

www.charliespeaking.com

Charlie@charliespeaking.com

There have been many influences throughout my career. Many people, co-workers, groups, teams, loved ones, liked ones, disliked ones and even make believe characters have contributed to my success.

I say thank you to all:

From the past:

The Beatles, Muhammad Ali, The Yankees, Dorothy, The Magnificent Seven, Kane, Linda Lobosco, My parents, Al Delgardo, Ed Butler, Fran, Helen Wyatt, Mary Flanagan, Larry Wilson, Lem Jones, John Lennon, Paul Divirgilio, Brian Bouten, Lynn Fox, Steve Czuchta, Gino Pandolfi, Renee Comack, Giancarlo Brandoni, Peggy Hoffman, Marshall Hutenberg, Jim Burns, Connell McGee, Richard Koslowski, Bob Szypula, Barry Wall, the quiet Beatle, John Gobinski, Marcus Kirkman, Charlie Baier, the Corleone family, Grace Slick, and Paul Kantner.

From the Fastpitch Softball coaching years:

Jess, Ali, Ashly, Kerri, Tara, Jill, Erin, Nicole, Tom Petillo (where are you these days?), all 4 Pagans, Craig Simon, The Meachams, The Gillhooleys, Mr. & Mrs. John Smith, The Pilons (really miss and think about Rick), the Finos, Eli, Brealand, Dave and Casey Halloran, and everyone that played for the Comets, the Clash and Charlie's Angels.

From the present:

The core four, Angelo, Mike B., Jay M., Lois E-H, Doug and Bernie, Martha, June Davidson, Vincent, Patricia and Caitlin Lobosco, the Internet, the Indigo Girls and all my friends in Chicago, Blue Ash and Cincinnati.

Of course Eva! Please remember my life is in your hands!

And to Carolyn and Christen: I love you both. As Emily sings, "A moment of peace is worth all of the wars behind us."

www.ingramcontent.com/pod-product-compliance
Lightning Source LLC
Chambersburg PA
CBHW032007170526
45157CB00002B/586